Scott Brown

Cartoonist

Fig. 1: Scott Brown, Brown's Soda Shop, Mansfield, Ohio, 1944

Scott Brown

Cartoonist

by

Christopher A. Kuntz

TURAS Publishing
Life is a Journey

Photo Credits:
Courtesy of the Richland County Historical Society, front and back cover images, Figs. 10, 52-57, 60, 62-63, 86-88, 90, 106, 108.
© J. Bruce Baumann – USA TODAY NETWORK, Fig. 44.
Scott Brown Collection, Billy Ireland Cartoon Library & Museum, Ohio State University, Figs. 7, 31-38, 45, 61, 107, 122.
Courtesy of *Collier's*, Figs. 47, 95-96.
Laff-A-Day © 1948 King Features Syndicate, Inc, Fig. 93.
Courtesy of the Mad River and NKP Railroad Museum, Bellevue, Ohio, Fig. 18.
Mansfield News Journal, Figs. 11-12, 94, 101, 126.
Mansfield Soldiers & Sailors Memorial Building and Museum, Figs. 114, 116-117.
Used with permission of *The Old Farmer's Almanac*/Almanac.com, Fig. 78.
Courtesy of *Outdoors Magazine*, Fig. 104.
Richland County Museum, Figs. 79-82, 84-85, 89.
Courtesy of *Richland Source*, Figs. 6, 16, 83.
© SEPS, Licensed by Curtis Licensing, Indianapolis, IN, Figs. 46, 59, 92, 97.

Scott Brown

Cartoonist

by

Christopher A. Kuntz

ScottBrownCartoonist@gmail.com

Cover Design by the Author

Editing and book interior design by Theresa Marie Flaherty

ISBN: 978-1-7361884-2-2 (Hardback)

🍀**TURAS** Publishing
4833 Saratoga Blvd., No. 129
Corpus Christi, TX 78413

for my mother, Barbara Brown Koons,
and for my children

Table of Contents

List of Figures ix

Introduction 1

BOOK I 3

    Chapter 1 Children of Pioneers 5

    Chapter 2 Frontier 9

    Chapter 3 Richland County, Ohio, May 20, 1870 25

    BOOK II 27

    Chapter 4 Hugh Maurice Brown 29

    Chapter 5 Scott Brown 33

    Chapter 6 The Largest, Coldest and Best Chocolate Soda on Route 30 83

Acknowledgments 85

Appendix A Ancestors of Robert and Sara Ledlie Brown 87

Appendix B Descendants of Robert and Sara Ledlie Brown 89

Endnotes 91

Bibliography 95

Index 97

About the Author 101

List of Figures

1. Scott Brown at the Soda shop frontispiece . . . . frontispiece
2. The Brown homestead today xiv
3. Linocut: "Feeding time," Scott Brown 3
4. Scott Brown at the entrance to the soda shop 5
5. B&O Crossing the Clear Fork River, Bellville, Ohio. 6
6. Image from a $5 Bill, Mansfield Bank, early 1800s. 9
7. Gristmill, Howard Scott Brown 10
8. Original land grant for the Brown homestead. 12
9. 1808 Map of Ohio 13
10. Early map of Richland County 13
11. Cartoon: "Early settlers feared wild animals" 14
12. Cartoon: "The good old days" 15
13. Detail from a *Famous Firsts* Poster 17
14. Newman Cabin, Richland County 18
15. Mary Gailey Brown 19
16. Early bank note, Mansfield 20
17. Two canals connect Lake Erie with the Ohio River 21
18. Painting: early train, artist unknown 23
19. Richland County 24
20. Hugh Maurice Brown. 27
21. Hugh and Nora's house, Mansfield, Ohio 29
22. Brown Brothers Hardware Store, Loudenville, Ohio 31
23. Mechanicsburg newspaper advertisement 32
24. Mechanicsburg, Ohio 32
25. Howard Scott Brown, ten weeks old 33
26. Howard Scott Brown 33
27. Hugh and Nora Steltz Brown 34
28. Nora Steltz Brown 35
29. Nora and granddaughter Barbara 35
30. Brown's Soda Shop 35
31: Sketchbook 36
32. Sketchbook 37
33. Sketchbook 38
34. Sketchbook 38
35. Drawing 39

List of Figures - *continued*

36. Drawing 39
37: Sketchbook 40
38. *La Scandler* Lampoon, front page 41
39. Untitled painting 41
40. Watercolor 41
41. Oil painting, undated 42
42. Oil painting, 1925 43
43. Oil painting, 1926 43
44. Scott Brown in the Soda Shop, 1964 44
45. Eighth grade report card 44
46. Cartoon: Original master 45
47. Cartoon: Original master 45
48. Cartoon: Original master 45
49. Cartoon: Original master 45
50. High School Senior Picture, 1927 46
51. *Habeus Corpses*, Chicago, 1929 46
52. Detail from a *Corner Parade* 47
53. Detail from a *Corner Parade* 47
54. Detail from a *Corner Parade* 47
55. Detail from a *Corner Parade* 48
56. Detail from a *Famous Firsts*, circa 1958 48
57. Detail from a *Corner Parade* 48
58. Cartoon: "Lost kite" 49
59. Cartoon: "Sharp tools" 49
60. The first *Corner Parade* poster, 1930 50
61. *The Passing Show* by Billy Ireland, 1915 50
62. Banner from the First *Corner Parade*, April 20, 1930 51
63. Banner from a *Corner Parade*, April 27, 1930 51
64. *Famous Firsts* 51
65. *Famous Firsts* 52
66. Scott Brown in the Soda Shop, circa 1944 52
67. Soda Shop Menu Cover 53
68. Soda Shop Menu 53
69. Two wooden Indians adorned the entrance to the store 53
70. Scott Brown's business name was Wooden Indian Studios 53

List of Figures - *continued*

71. Scott Brown self portrait, circa 1945 54
72. Anna Von Endt Brown 55
73. Anna Von Endt Brown 55
74. Daughters Barbara and Linda with Scott Brown in his studio. 55
75. Barbara and Linda Brown 55
76. "The Rabbits' Nest" 56
77. Scott Brown's snow predictions, 1958-1973 57
78. Old Farmer's Almanac 1975. 58
79. Cartoon: Seymour Lindsey fools William Ledlie Brown 59
80. Portrait of Seymour Lindsey, undated 60
81. Paper Cutout, Seymour Lindsey 60
82. Wooden post detail, Seymour Lindsey, unknown date 60
83. Oil painting, Seymout Lindsey, unknown date 60
84. Cartoon: "Seymour Lindsey made time for kids". 61
85. Cartoon: "Seymour Lindsey paints the pews". 61
86. Cartoon: Detail draft #1 62
87. Cartoon: Detail draft #2 62
88. Cartoon: Detail draft #3 62
89. Cartoon: Final comic detail 62
90. Detail from a *Corner Parade* 63
91. Scott Brown, circa 1940 63
92. Cartoon: "I didn't say it was a small diamond" 64
93. Cartoon: "This isn't MY purse!" 64
94. Cartoon: "Municipal government". 64
95. Cartoon: "Our need is rather urgent". 65
96. Cartoon: "Blowing it all in" 65
97. Cartoon: "We thought you weren't going to stop" 65
98. Cartoon: Big Valentine card 66
99. Cartoon: Original master 66
100. Cartoon: Original master 66
101. Cartoon: Original master 67
102. Cartoon: "By golly, this batch is good!" 67
103. Cartoon: "Invite the boys" 67
104. Cartoon: "The fishing widow". 68
105. Scott Brown with dog 68

List of Figures - *continued*

106. Cartoon: Detail from a *Corner Parade* 68
107. Oil painting, unknown date 69
108. Oil painting, unknown date 69
109. Fountain drawing, approximately age ten 69
110. Put-in-Bay, 1925 69
111. Brooch, oil on wood 70
112. Vasbinder Fountain (oil), 1936 70
113. Linocut, Vasbinder Fountain, circa 1958 71
114. Linocut with color added, Vasbinder Fountain, circa 1958 71
115: Detail from a *Corner Parade* 72
116. Low relief sculpture: "Johnny Appleseed ". 72
117. Low relief sculpture "Deer in the woods" 72
118. Birthday card 73
119. Birthday card 73
120. Christmas card: "Boy, what a Christmas!" 74
121. Christmas card: "Jet propelled angels" 75
122. Christmas card: "Out on my ass" 76
123. Handcrafted toys, 1970s 77
124. Groundhog Day card, 1967 78
125. Groundhog Day card, 1965 78
126. Cartoon: "Groundhog Day," 1969 79
127. Gag newspaper from the Soda Shop 80
128. Thank you card 80
129. Thank you card 80
130. Howard Scott Brown 81
131. Painting, Scott Brown, 1971 84
132. Christopher A. Kuntz 101

One who is anciently aware of existence
Is master of every moment

- Lao Tzu

Fig. 2: The Brown Homestead today
Photograph by the author

Introduction

Scott Brown, my grandfather, was a nationally known cartoonist and the proprietor of Brown's Soda Shop in Mansfield, Ohio, from the 1920s through the 1960s. Just about anyone who grew up in Mansfield a generation ago remembers him fondly for his cartoons, weather predictions, and chocolate sodas.

Although this is a book about Scott Brown, to fully appreciate him means getting to know his father, Hugh Maurice Brown. Scott Brown spent every day, all day, by his father's side from the time he was a young child at the H. M. Brown Grain Company in Mechanicsburg, Ohio, through his adolescence and adult life at Brown's Soda Shop in Mansfield.

Hugh Maurice Brown grew up on the Brown homestead near the town of Lexington, just south of Mansfield. The homestead was founded shortly after the War of 1812 by pioneers Robert and Sara Ledlie Brown. After his mother's death when he was just two, Hugh was raised collectively by many of the thirty children and grandchildren of the pioneers.

The pioneer history that so deeply affected his father is woven intimately into Scott Brown's artwork and cartoons.

This is where his story begins.

Christopher A. Kuntz

Note: Readers are encouraged to visit www.scottbrowncartoonist.com for extensive genealogical information regarding the ancestors and descendents of Robert and Sara Ledlie Brown. The website also contains more images and further discussion of many of the topics in this book.

BOOK I

Fig. 3: "Feeding Time" Linocut, Scott Brown, circa 1958

Chapter 1

Children of Pioneers

1969

When I was a kid, I loved to visit my grandfather's soda shop at the corner of Helen and Fourth in Mansfield, Ohio, on warm summer days. I skipped up the sidewalk, through the corner door, greeted the wooden Indian, and jumped up to the counter, swinging my feet and spinning the barstool. On the wall behind the bar hung a large pair of antlers. While my grandfather mixed me up a chocolate soda, I searched for anything new and exciting on the cluttered and colorful wall. The narrow aisles revealed a treasure trove of balsa wood airplanes, whoopee cushions, fake turds, gum, lifesavers, and Coca Cola.

The house where my grandparents lived, and my mom grew up, was located a block and a half from the store. The doorframes stood at odd angles, and the floors creaked with every step. The faint, sweet, pleasant smell of old cigar smoke faded from awareness after awhile. The stairs were narrow and far too steep, and the rooms at the top so small a double bed hardly allowed one to pass on three sides.

In the upstairs bathroom, tiny hexagonal black and white tiles made fascinating patterns on the floor and counter. Cracks snaked their way through the patterns. The porcelain sink handles squeaked, and the water tasted cold and sweet.

The dining room was barely large enough for a table seating four. Above the finest piece of furniture in the house—a chest of drawers—hung a painting my grandfather created in 1939:

Fig. 4: Scott Brown at the entrance to the Soda Shop, circa 1940

Fig. 5: B&O Crossing the Clear Fork River, Bellville, Ohio, 1939

The painting occupied the most important display space in the house. My grandfather chose the theme carefully. Transportation was critical to the emergence of Richland County from the frontier wilderness homesteaded by our pioneer ancestors, to the community that existed when he painted this picture over one hundred years later.

The painting features horse-drawn cart, train, and river. The farmer and his cart move quietly away from the train and the factory. Smoke rises into the air. The old and new move in opposite directions; and the most ancient of all, the river, is in between.

This view is from a small hill looking south over the Clear Fork River just outside of Bellville on the afternoon of a fall day in 1939.[1] Hundreds of generations of Native Americans navigated by canoe from this location through the dense forests all the way to the Ohio River without a single portage. In the early 1800s, Euro-American pioneers traveled the same route on flatboats laden with goods.

Back in my grandfather's house, a classic German barometer hung on the wall above the kitchen table. Two characters rotated in and out of a house according to the weather. This was his favorite kind of barometer, not so much because of its accuracy, but because of the visual effect of one or the other figure coming out of the house to predict the weather. It kept things interesting.

Out back were tomatoes and many bird feeders that were always full.

Chapter 2

Frontier

Fig. 6: Image from a $5 Bill, Mansfield Bank, early 1800s. Courtesy of the <u>Richland Source</u>.

Richland County, Ohio, 1812

In the spring of 1812, Amariah Watson crossed the Old Boundary Line on his way north to occupy a cabin he built the year before on the Clear Fork River, near what is now the front lawn of the Lexington Cemetery.

What the locals called the Old Boundary Line was more widely known as the Greenville Treaty Line. It was the border of the United States until very recently. North of the line was Indian country. Watson's cabin did not have windows. Instead, the cabin was dimly lit by blockhouse-style portholes, designed to defend against attack.

Watson had scouted out a short v-shaped valley where the Clear Fork River cut through a small rise in an otherwise relatively flat river plain. The shape of this valley was ideal for building a sawmill. The sawmill was necessary to build a gristmill.

Watson was anxious to get his wife and three young children settled in their wilderness home before she gave birth to their fourth child. The baby came two weeks after they got there.

Shortly after Watson's arrival, the War of 1812 began, increasing tensions between the Indians and settlers in northern Ohio. Suspicion and fear exploded on August 16, 1812, when U.S. General William Hull inexplicably surrendered Fort Detroit to an inferior British force. Northern Ohio was suddenly utterly exposed to the British and their Indian allies.

The surrender came like a clap of thunder from a clear sky,...[2]

Pioneers and militia frantically built blockhouses all along the Ohio frontier over the course of just a few days. These blockhouses—tiny wooden castles—were the U.S Army and Militia's forward outposts and site of refuge for the settlers during the tense years of the War of 1812. Everybody knew where to find the closest blockhouse.

In spite of the war, Watson managed to have the sawmill running in the fall of 1812. He built the gristmill in 1814, knowing that the gristmill would draw settlers to the region.

Euro-American settlement of the Ohio frontier in the early 1800s happened one small river at a time: sawmill, gristmill, roads, and then settlers. Watson's gristmill on the Clear Fork River was the beginning of the town of Lexington.

Fig. 7: Gristmill
Howard Scott Brown, circa 1925 (age fifteen).
Scott Brown Collection, Billy Ireland Cartoon Library & Museum, Ohio State University.

Robert Brown

One of the first pioneers to be attracted by Watson's mill was Robert Brown. Robert had his eyes on the Ohio frontier from the moment he arrived on the *Abolus* out of Newry, Ireland, in December 1811.[3] His siblings had other ideas. Robert's sisters went on to establish large clans in civilized country east of the Ohio River around Pittsburgh and Philadelphia. Mary had twelve children; Elizabeth had six. Robert's older brother, James, returned to Ireland where he had five children. His brother, William, married twice and also had five children.

On December 3, 1814—just months after Watson's gristmill began operating—Robert made the down payment on one-hundred-sixty acres of land located about two miles east of Watson's mill. He paid $2 per acre, the same price Watson paid in 1812.[4]

When Robert made this investment, America was at war with the British, and part of the war had to do with who controlled Ohio. If the Americans lost the war, any investment Robert made in Ohio would also be lost. In retrospect, Robert's timing was phenomenal. Although he could not have known it at the time, the Treaty of Ghent ending the war was signed in Belgium on December 24, 1814, just three weeks after Robert made his downpayment.

It appears that the first time Robert actually visited Ohio was in 1816, a year after the end of the war. He certainly visited Watson's mill. After exploring the sparsely populated wilderness around Richland County, Robert returned to the town of Kings Creek in the picturesque hills on the eastern banks of the Ohio River. Kings Creek, near present day Weirton, West Virginia, was at the edge of civilized country. This is where the young immigrant with a charming Irish accent encountered Sara Ledlie.

Sara Ledlie

In monumental contrast to Robert, Sara had never known anything *other* than the frontier. Sara's mother, Mary Lusk Andrews Ledlie, was born in 1745. She was a third-generation American whose grandparents were among the earliest Scots-Irish immigrants to the Colonies. They came to America in 1721.

Mary Lusk Andrews Ledlie was married twice. David Andrews, her first husband and the father of her first eight children, was killed in 1782 on the Crawford Expedition. She raised her children in Kings Creek as a widow for four years before marrying William Ledlie. They had three additional children, the last of whom was Sara.

William Ledlie was a teacher and considered a "man of education and weight in his day."[5] He immigrated to America from Ireland as a young man, most likely in the 1760s.

Sara Ledlie and Robert Brown married in Brook County, West Virginia, on April 17, 1817. Sara was twenty-three-years old, Robert twenty-seven. They were surely a handsome couple. Sara was a big woman who spoke frontier Virginia drawl; the eleventh child of a woman whose family had lived on the frontier for the last hundred years. Robert grew up across the Atlantic Ocean in the shadows of castles and bridges built before the beginning of time. Ireland was as distant as another planet. Although Robert and Sara spoke English in different tongues and came from different upbringings, they were united in their Scots-Irish ancestry and Presbyterian faith.

On March 8, 1819, more than four years after his down payment and seven years after arriving in America, Robert paid off his Richland County investment and received a grant for the land signed by U.S. President Monroe.

Robert and Sara were living in Kings Creek when they received the grant. Their first child was about a year old, and Sara was pregnant with their second. This may be why another two years passed before they occupied the homestead.

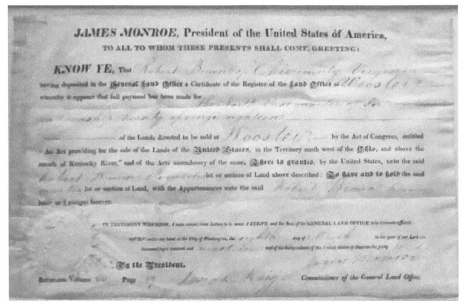

Fig. 8: Original land grant for the Brown homestead

In 1821, most likely in the spring, Robert, Sara, and their two young children Nancy and Margaret crossed the Ohio River on their way to Richland County. They traveled the dirt road by foot and wagon.

They crossed the Ohio River a few miles south of Kings Creek at Mingo Bottom, near the current town of Steubenville. Their one-hundred-twenty-mile trip took weeks. They travelled southwest through Cadiz, crossed the Tuscawaras Valley, and passed through the hamlets of New Philadelphia, Wooster, and then straight west to Mansfield.

They followed paths that had been used by Indians for thousands of years. These paths were widened during the American Revolution and developed further during the War of 1812.[6] Now, just six years after the war, the cut marks on the trees were still fresh. Military debris lay rusting alongside the road.

The streams were swollen with spring rain. They passed huge mounds, which they knew were created by a civilization that had thrived on this land for hundreds of generations—and then vanished.

At some point they crossed the Greenville Treaty Line. Once north of this line, they were on land that belonged to the Indians according to the Greenville Treaty of 1795. A series of treaties over the next several decades progressively restricted their lands. The Indians were forced out. By the time the War of 1812 ended, very few Indians were left in Richland County.

The Brown homestead was about two miles east of Watson's mill on a relatively high point. The rolling hills were swampy in some places; wooded in others.

The Browns probably built a temporary shelter adequate for the summer months. This could be done in a day, allowing the pioneers to begin immediately the task of clearing fields and putting in crops. They waited until the fall to build their cabin.

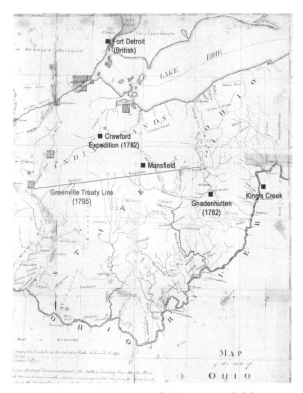

Fig. 9: 1808 Map of Ohio - Mansfield is north of the Greenville Treaty Line

Sara was well adapted to the frontier:

She (Sara Ledlie Brown) is the ideal type of the pioneer, having force of character, strong of nerve, athletic and in her pristine days weighed 208 pounds and wielded the ax with vigor and zest in subduing the forest for her cabin home.[7]

Robert and Sara's oldest child Nancy was three when the family arrived. Her experience was probably similar to that of John Leedy, who arrived in Richland County a few years before her:

I was 4 years old when my father settled here. We stopped right in the wood, built an Indian shed of bark and forks, slept for a time in our wagons, and lived in this way until September. In September we built our cabin.

Wild animals were plenty. We had difficulty to keep the wolves from killing old dog Bounce. We frequently had to get up and chase them from our wigwam and wagon. Bears, deer, wild cats, coons, o'possums, skunks, rattlesnakes, copperheads, and snakes generally, were plenty, together with a few panthers....[9]

Sara never took her eyes off her children. And for a good reason.

Black snakes, rattlesnakes and other varieties of the reptile were everywhere in the woods, the swamps, the clearings, by the trail, in the yard, often in the house and sometimes in the beds....[8]

Not just in the beds, but in the schools:

The first school was taught by Polly Braden in 1818, in a log house with a split floor.... Whilst the teacher was engaged in prayer at the close of school one evening, a rattlesnake was observed by some of the pupils raising its head up through a crack in the floor, but no one dared move till the prayer was completed.....[10]

A giant rattlesnake was rumored to inhabit a particular Richland County swamp:

Fig. 10: Early map of Richland County - The location of the Brown Homestead has been added. Courtesy of the Richland County Historical Society.

This was a terrifying creature up to 15 feet long and with horny spines along its back. It allegedly fed on sheep and hogs and was heard bellowing from the swamp on dark nights....[11]

For some, this was just a fairy tale. For others...

In 1858 when Allen B. Beverstock bought a 120-acre tract in the swampy area he wanted to be sure the big snake was included in his purchase so it was mentioned in the deed and a drawing of the big rattler appeared on the deed.[12]

It wasn't just the snakes. Raising sheep was almost impossible because of the wolves. Large, aggressive bears went after the pigs. Lead balls from previous encounters were often found in bears that were killed.

Fig. 11: "Early settlers feared wild animals" by Scott Brown.[13] Courtesy of the <u>Mansfield News Journal</u>.

Robert and Sara built their homestead in the wilderness under these conditions while caring for two very young children. And they created another child within weeks of their arrival. As frost dusted their first crops in the fall of 1821, they prepared for a February birth.

Although they were among the earliest arrivals in Richland County, Robert and Sara were not alone. They had help from other settlers clearing their fields and building their cabin, and they helped others as well.

Grandfather Brown (Robert Brown) owned a loom and wove, not only for their own family, but for neighbors. When the people were much in need of cloth, grandma would weave until midnight, then her husband would rise and weave until morning.[14]

Fig. 12: "The good old days" by Scott Brown. Courtesy of the <u>Mansfield News Journal</u>.

A. A. Graham, in his sentinel 1870 work, *History of Richland County,* describes the pioneers:

> *There was no punctilious formality, no aping after fashions. The rich and poor were dressed alike. The clothing of the men consisted of coarse material for hunting shirts, and pants made of buckskin. The women were attired in coarse fabric....[15]*

Graham continues:

> *The early settlers were a rough, hardy set of backwoodsmen; and, if they are always ready for a fight, they were also always ready to help each other on any and all occasions, and for this purpose would put themselves to great inconvenience and go great distances. Did one of them want a cabin raised, he had only to let his neighbors (and all were neighbors who lived within a circle of five or ten miles) know they were wanted on a certain day, and they would be there, the only compensation asked being a generous supply of whisky.[16]*

Whiskey was an everyday part of life. Apart from its generous local use, whiskey was about the only profitable commodity. The central role of whiskey to the daily life of early settlements is evident in this description of the founding of the town of Paris, just north of Mansfield, shortly after the War of 1812:

Very soon after the town was laid out, Abraham Trux erected the gristmill and a sawmill near his house, on a branch of the Huron River. Two distilleries were also erected, one by Lemuel Powers and the other by William McKelvey. These distilleries purchased the corn, which they made into whisky, and therefore created a market for corn, about the only article of produce the farmer could sell. The whisky was hauled to the lake where it found a ready market—except what was consumed at home, which was no small quantity.[17]

Whiskey was a lubricant when trading with the Indians. At least in part because of whiskey, a good fight was common at any large gathering except church. Whiskey was the expected reward for helping with a barn raising or log rolling.

One of Richland County's earliest citizen organizations was the Washington and Monroe Temperance Society, formed on March 29, 1828. Its statement of purpose:

We, whose names are hereunto attached, do pledge ourselves
to dispense with the common use of ardent spirits in our families,
and at our gatherings and frolics,
and as far as our influence extends,
use all laudable means to discourage the use of it in others.[18]

This was adopted only after considerable discussion among the members of the nascent society, who feared that attaching their names to such a dour mission statement would prevent them from attracting neighbors to their log rollings.

And they were right. It was only a short time before the first *Anti*-Temperance Society appeared. Their pledge was simple:

Help no man raise, roll, or harvest without liquor[19]

The Temperance Society had little impact on the role that whiskey played on the Richland County economy or social structure. Distilleries were commonplace.

In one township alone there were no less than six in full blast at one time. Whiskey was currency for which grain was exchanged. It was a common beverage among all classes, a social habit....[20]

One of the most famous drinkers in early Richland County was Abram Steltz, great-grandfather of Scott Brown on his mother's side. A veteran of the War of 1812, Abram worked and fought as hard as he drank. He was said to have fists the size of sledgehammers and had as many enemies as he had friends. The following event occurred when he was eighty-four years old:

Last week Abram Steltz split 1,000 rails. One half of a large cut rolled back when it opened and caught him under it. He undertook to dig out with his hands and succeeded very well until he came to frozen ground. He then yelled so loud that two men came to his rescue and extracted him. He deliberately went back to work and finished his job.[21]

Abram lived on forty acres of land given to him and his bride Catherine Weaver by her parents when she married him against their wishes. It was on this land that he discovered gold—or rather, gold discovered him.

One afternoon he was drunk as a skunk and fell face first with a giant splash into a stream on his property. Neighbors came to his assistance when they heard him cussing and clawing his way up the bank and saw his britches and beard were glittering, igniting a frantic local gold rush that netted about a thimbleful of the precious metal.[22]

When he died in 1878, his obituary stated:

> *Mr. Steltz was one of the toughest and most robust men, and did a heap of hard, pioneer labor, but on account of using liquor too freely he accumulated only a little property.*[23]

Fig. 13: Detail from a "Famous Firsts" Poster, 1931, by Scott Brown

The cabin Robert and Sara built in the fall of 1821 was probably about fourteen-by-sixteen feet on the inside, and similar to the early Richland County cabin described below:

> *... a little log pen, with a roof over it; a wide fireplace occupying nearly all of one end, with a stick and mud chimney running up on the outside, no floor but mother earth; windows made of a little twelve-by-twelve piece of oiled paper, put in where a log was sawed off for the purpose. It contained but a single room with a loft overhead; was made of rough, round beech logs with the bark on, chinked and daubed with sticks and mud to keep out the wintry blast.[24]*

Fig. 14: Newman Cabin, Richland County, 1808

On the day of a cabin raising, laughter, conversation, and the sound of chopping wood echoed in the valleys. The September air smelled of falling leaves, pumpkins, roasting meat, and apple cider. A fiddle emerged at sunset as the pioneers relaxed around the fire, warmed themselves with whiskey, and admired their day's work.

Robert and Sara chose a protected site about fifty feet below the ridge, just above a spring. The site of the original cabin is still visible as a flattening of a mild grade, and the spring is still flowing.[25]

This cabin is likely where William Ledlie Brown— Scott Brown's grandfather—was born on February 28, 1822, as the young family emerged from their first winter in Richland County. The young couple and three small children lived in the single-room cabin with a fireplace at one end and storage above the main cabin.

William's sister-in-law, Mary Gailey Brown, described William's early years in a speech she gave almost a century later at the 1908 Brown family reunion:

Fig. 15: Mary Gailey Brown

His (William Ledlie Brown) cradle was a sugar trough. Wild animals were still to be seen….We all know the story of grandmother (Sara Ledlie) riding through the woods on horseback, between Sandy Hill and the farm, carrying fresh meat, and hearing wolves howling on her track. Malaria was rife from new soil and undrained swamps, and the pioneers often shook for weeks with ague. Quinine was unknown as a remedy, and they relied upon boneset or other bitter herbs for medicine and shook until frost congealed the source of malaria. Acres of heavy timber were felled and being of no commercial value, these logs were rolled into great heaps and burned. They manufactured nearly everything for their own use—even their clothing—the women spinning both flax and wool, and the cloth woven on hand looms.

These pioneers brought with them to the wilderness the piety of their Scotch-Irish ancestors. The Sabbath was strictly observed, and public worship attended when possible, the mother and father taking day [sic] about going to church, often carrying children with them on horseback.

When our ancestors came to Richland county, feed was so scarce in spring, that trees were cut down so that cattle might browse on the tender twigs, and during one severe snowstorm in spring, people emptied straw beds to feed cattle. The facilities for work were most primitive. Where now we cook on steel ranges, or put a match to natural gas, our pioneer mothers cooked for barn raisings and log rollings on open fires, with outside chimneys built with sticks and mud. Sickles, and cradles were used in harvesting the crops in the stumpy fields.[26]

The homesteaders grew corn and wheat, and most likely raised chickens, turkeys, cattle, and pigs. Tilling the fields and moving logs was done with horses; trees were cut down with handsaws and axes. Candles, oil lamps, the fireplace, and the moon provided light at night.

Clearing the land by hand took years. When they could produce more grain than they needed, Robert and Sara likely hauled it downhill to Watson's mills for processing into flour and whiskey. They probably also raised cattle and pigs for market.

One barrier to accruing wealth was a lack of currency. In the early 1800s, there was no currency in Ohio backed by the U.S. government. Silver was used when possible, but barter was more common. Amariah Watson extracted a portion of the gristmill's product as payment for his service.[27] "Wildcat Banks" printed currency that, although beautiful, was worth as much as the paper it was printed on when the banks failed.

And eventually they all did. The situation was particularly dire a few years after the end of the War of 1812. The demand by the military for local grain vanished, resulting in financial panic.[28] This regional financial collapse occurred in 1819, the same year that Robert Brown paid off his investment and took ownership of his land.

Fig. 16: Early bank note, Mansfield. Courtesy of the <u>Richland Source</u>.

Transportation was another formidable barrier. The products of the land could only be moved to market over primitive roads or by river. The overland trail passed north through Mansfield to the mouth of the Huron River on Lake Erie. Giant covered wagons with wheels eight-inches broad and an inch thick, requiring six horses, transported goods along this forty-eight-mile route.[29] The trip took about a week. The wagons shared this route with farmers driving pigs, turkeys, and cattle to market. In the summer, travelers choked on the dust. In the winter, they arrived smelling of livestock sweat and excrement.

Goods could also be moved by river. Mansfield was located at the highest part of the divide between Lake Erie to the north and the Ohio River to the south. It was possible to navigate a flatboat all the way to the Ohio River, with a single portage—a dam above Loudonville.

Once on the Ohio River, goods could then be floated to New Orleans, where they were sold along with the boat. The return to Ohio was by foot, with the round trip lasting ninety days.[30]

In the 1820s and 1830s, two north-south canals were built in Ohio, but one was too far east and the other too far west to benefit Richland County. The canals skirted the region widely due to its altitude.

The Ohio Canal System

Fig. 17: In the 1830s, two canals connected Lake Erie with the Ohio River. The blue dot shows the location of the Brown homestead.

The canals enriched the corridors they served—and left Richland County further behind. In 1836, plans were made for a steep east-west canal with eight locks connecting Mansfield with the Ohio and Erie canal to the east. The proposed waterway was called the *Mohican and Black Fork Canal*. The project was set back by the financial crisis of 1837, and then abandoned because of the advent of the train a few years later.[31] Serious consideration of such a formidable project demonstrates how desperate the region was for transportation.

Another missing piece of infrastructure was law and order. Hideouts in the forks of the Mohican were home to bands of highwaymen, horse thieves, and counterfeiters who preyed on travelers and the local population. Among the best-documented Richland County brigands were John Driskill and the Driskill-Brodie gang, who were active during the 1820s to mid 1830s.

Driskill was apprehended more than once and escaped confinement several times. In 1827, posters appeared a few miles east in Loudonville offering a $25 reward for his capture, stating:

Escaped from the custody of the subscriber….a certain JOHN DRISKILL, light complexion about 5 feet 10 inches high, supposed to be about 50 years old—a piece bit off his nose,...[32]

About Driskill's nose; he brought it upon himself. He chewed the ear off of a member of the Poe family during a fight. The Poe's were a pretty tough family. The fellow desired revenge. About a year after losing his ear, Poe busted through a phalanx of Driskill's gang and clamped his teeth around Driskill's nose before anyone knew what he was after.[33] No one ever found the missing piece.

Horse thieving was severely punished. The law demanded a minimum of fifty lashes and allowed up to two hundred for a single offense. Ears were cropped for a third offense. This is why Driskill's partner Brodie had no ears. The pair made quite a sight riding casually into Lexington side by side on a dusty summer afternoon.

Eventually the Driskill-Brodie band was just too unwelcome around Richland County. In 1835 some members of the gang fled to Rock River country in Illinois where they reappeared under a new name, the *Prairie Pirates.*[34]

Sara's mother Mary Lusk died in 1827. After only six years on the farm, the Browns moved back east across the Ohio River to Kings Creek to provide care and companionship for Sara's father William

Ledlie. In those six years, Robert and Sara had added William, Sara, and John to the two daughters they had originally brought to Richland County in 1821. Now, five children between one and ten years of age made the journey back to Kings Creek.

They stayed for seven years, until William Ledlie died in 1835. During their time in Kings Creek, Robert and Sara had another three children; James, Mary, and Robert Carson. Robert Carson Brown, their eighth and last child, was born less than a year before William Ledlie's death. The newborn child that the veteran of the Revolution held in his arms in the final months of his life was destined, decades later, to command the 64th Regiment of Ohio's Sherman Brigade in the Civil War.

In 1829 Ledlie sold two-hundred-fifty-one acres of land in the Kings Creek for one dollar to Robert Brown. This was prime land located at the confluence of Kings Creek and the Ohio River.[35] It was granted to Ledlie over forty years earlier in 1783.[36]

Robert and Sara now owned one-hundred-sixty acres on the frontier in Richland County and two-hundred-fifty-one acres on the eastern banks of the Ohio River in Kings Creek. Robert had a choice—and he chose the frontier. Robert and Sara sold the Kings Creek land for $448 in September 1835.[37] It is likely the money was invested in farm equipment, livestock, and years later, land in Iowa.

After William Ledlie's death, Robert and Sara returned to the Lexington homestead with their eight children ranging in age from one to eighteen. They never left the homestead again.

More settlers arrived while they were gone, but Richland County was still backcountry. The desirable land bordered the canals.

In 1833 Robert bought another 92.5 acres in Richland County for just $1.25 per acre—far less than the $2.00 per acre he paid for his first one-hundred-sixty acres a generation before.[38] This second purchase was during the height of the canal era.

When the economy collapsed in 1837, investing in Richland County land appeared to be a terrible idea. Then, in May 1846, a small steam engine named *Empire* rumbled slowly into the outskirts of Mansfield from the north pulling a short string of open train cars filled with people.[39] A large, cheering crowd greeted it. Everyone came to witness this monumental event. When the conductor blew the train whistle, horses bolted and people fainted.

Within a few years, the railroad continued south of Mansfield to Lexington (1850) and on to Newark. It became the Sandusky, Mansfield, and Newark Line, later a section of the B&O Railroad, now a bicycle trail.

The other engines were named *Richland, Knox, Bellville, Licking, Lexington,* and *Mansfield.* They had no lights. Traveling speed was about twelve miles an hour. A single small freight car, a mail car, and a passenger car carrying up to thirty people were typical. The conductor and team frequently stopped to cut wood for the engine. The trains ran on a single track and needed to pull over at intervals to let trains going in the opposite direction pass. Because this was before the telegraph, miscommunications were common, leading to "cornfield meets"—where two engines came cowcatcher to cowcatcher or perhaps even experienced a low speed collision.[40]

The tracks were made of wood topped with strap rail. The wood decayed and weather took its toll on the embankments. Derailments were common. Occasionally a piece of strap rail would dislodge and, with a huge bang, shoot up through the floor into the passenger or mail car, impaling whatever was in its way and stopping the train dead. This terrifying and sometimes lethal event was called a snakehead.[41]

Fig. 18: Courtesy of the Mad River and NKP Railroad Museum, Bellevue, Ohio.

Derailments, cornfield meets and snakeheads aside, the trip to Sandusky that once took a week could be done in a single day—without all the dust, mud, and stench. Trains became bigger and faster. Steel rails replaced wood and strap rail. Unlike the canals, trains could go almost anywhere and ship goods all year long. Two more railroads passed through Mansfield. Mansfield became the primary transportation hub of northern Ohio.

And the canals? Slow. Tough to maintain. Froze in the winter.

The impact of the railroads on commerce in Richland County can be inferred by following the values of land through time. In 1833, Robert Brown paid $1.25 per acre. By 1850 the value of this land had increased almost 20 times to $22 per acre.[42]

Robert's relatives in civilized country east of the Ohio River probably knitted their brows when he put the down payment on disputed land while the War of 1812 was still being fought. They might have sighed when the economy in the region crumbled in 1819, the year he paid off his investment. They probably said "I told you so" in the 1820s when canals became the state of the art in transportation, sucking business away from Richland County. They most likely were aghast when he sold the land in Kings Creek in 1835. And they must have concluded that he was completely, utterly out of his mind when he invested in another 92.5 acres, shortly before the financial panic of 1837. But as the *Empire* rumbled slowly into Mansfield in May of 1846, it became clear that Robert Brown, the visionary, had chosen some of the finest land in Ohio.

Fig. 19: Richland County, circa 1880 (artist unknown)

Chapter 3

Richland County, Ohio

May 20, 1870

It is five years after the end of the Civil War. The spring breeze on the Brown homestead east of the town of Lexington is fragrant from the flowers of giant apple trees, planted by the young pioneers when they arrived nearly fifty years before. Most of the land has been cleared for pasture and crops. Cattle roam the fields.

Elizabeth Ritchie Brown

In 1870, there were about thirty Browns living on the homestead spanning three generations, all descendants of Robert and Sara Ledlie Brown. Robert died a year before, but Sara, now seventy-seven-years old, was still a powerful force on the farm and an equal contributor to the work. Five of Robert and Sara's eight grown children lived on the farm with their spouses and families.

Elizabeth Ritchie Brown, the wife of eldest son William Ledlie Brown, was one of only two women caring for infants or toddlers. The other families had moved on from this phase of life. Elizabeth had six children and was pregnant again. Two of her children were still quite young; Edgar Milton was four, and Hugh Maurice was two. The others were adolescents.

The other woman with an infant was Mary Gailey Brown, the wife of Colonel Robert Carson Brown. She arrived just two years before when she wed the colonel in 1868, shortly after he returned from the South. Mary gave birth to their first child, Helen, less than a year later. At the age of thirty, she was quite old for a first-time mother. Because they were the only women with infants and toddlers and their husbands cooperated to run the farm, Elizabeth and Mary were certainly close companions.

Elizabeth, thirty-nine, had given birth to eight children in eighteen years (two had died as infants). A walking encyclopedia about pregnancy, childbirth, and child rearing, she was an excellent mentor. Mary anticipated raising Helen and probably more children in the supportive company of her experienced sister-in-law.

But that is not how things turned out. On May 20, 1870, just weeks after giving birth to her seventh living child, Elizabeth Ritchie Brown died. Among the seven children who lost their mother that day were the newborn, Charles Alexander, and two toddlers; Edgar Milton and Hugh Maurice.

Mary Gailey Brown suddenly found herself playing a central role raising Elizabeth's three now motherless little ones—while nursing her own infant.

The needs of these three little boys might explain why Mary did not have another child (Charles Gailey Brown) for four years. It might explain why William Ledlie Brown's oldest child Anne, who was eighteen when Elizabeth died, continued to live on the farm and did not marry for eight years.

And perhaps it provides some insight into Edgar Milton Brown. Edgar was four when his mother died. Just before he was born, he also lost a sister, Addie Maggie, who would have been two years older than him. She died of cholera. Edgar later became an influential physician, city council member, and Presbyterian elder in Zanesville. A man of seemingly limitless energy, he was a passionate advocate for public health, clean water, and maternal-fetal health.

Almost forty years after Elizabeth's death Mary Gailey Brown gave the keynote speech at the 1908 Brown Reunion. Perhaps she was thinking of her sister-in-law Elizabeth when she said:

> *We appear, we play our little part, and some sooner, some later, leave the stage to be occupied by others. Every man is useful, but no man is essential, and no matter how important we think ourselves to be, we must give place to others.*[43]

The person most affected by Elizabeth Ritchie Brown's death was Hugh Maurice Brown. Hugh's mother vanished from his life suddenly, inexplicably, unjustly, and forever when he was just two years old and beginning to utter his first words.

BOOK II

Fig. 20: Hugh Maurice Brown

Chapter 4

Hugh Maurice Brown

Fig. 21: Hugh and Nora's house, Mansfield, Ohio, 1918.
Scott Brown and Hugh Maurice Brown are sitting on the lawn.

*T*he house was a high, white, Victorian bride, scrolls and swirls, spindles and gingerbread, with a white veranda that swept around two sides like a full tiered wedding gown. It stood triumphant on the green carpet of summer, all lace and celebration, wreathed in sunlight, and roses, and bees humming in honeysuckle.[44]

Barbara Koons, daughter of Scott Brown

Hugh Maurice Brown, the sixth living child of Elizabeth Ritchie and William Ledlie Brown, and one of over forty grandchildren of pioneers Sara Ledlie and Robert Brown, was born on the Brown homestead in 1868, shortly after the Civil War. The tragedy of his mother's death when he was barely two was replaced by the fortune of being raised by dozens of brothers, sisters, aunts, uncles, cousins, and his venerable grandmother, Sara Ledlie Brown.

When he was twenty-one Hugh left the farm to work in the hardware business in Bellville, a few miles to the south. His older brother by nine years, John Thomas Brown, worked in a hardware store in Bellville as well. No doubt they worked together.

Hugh met Nora Steltz, Abram Steltz's granddaughter, at a Bellville dance. The two later married.

In 1895, the couple moved about twenty miles east to Loudonville, where Hugh established Brown Brothers Hardware Store with his little brother Charles. Hugh was twenty-seven; Nora was twenty. Their daughter, Lucille, was born in the fall of 1898. Charles and his wife Sylvia's daughter, Mable, was born a month earlier. The girls spent their first seven years side by side.

The brothers and the store are described in the *1901 Centennial Biographical History of Richland and Ashland Counties, Ohio*:

> *These gentlemen (Hugh Maurice Brown and Charles Alexander Brown) constitute the well-known firm of Brown Brothers, dealers in hardware in Loudonville. They occupy an enviable position in business circles and are active promoters of the commercial activity whereon depend the advancement, progress, and prosperity of every community. They were both natives of Richland County, born at the family home south of Mansfield....*
>
> *...from 1889 to 1895 he (Hugh Maurice Brown) was engaged in the hardware business at Bellville, Richland county, but in the latter year he came to Loudonville, where he was joined by his brother in the establishment of Brown Brothers, hardware merchants. They have a good store, well stocked with everything found in their line and now enjoy a large trade, which has been conducted upon honorable business methods, courtesy and prompt attention being shown to all their patrons.*
>
> *The brothers and their wives are all prominent, well-known people of Loudonville, where they have gained a large circle of friends....Their attention, however, is largely given to business affairs and they have found that enterprise and diligence form a sure path to success. Both are members of the Knights of Pythias fraternity, in politics are staunch Democrats and in religion are members of the Presbyterian Church.[45]*

Another description of the brothers and the store was written around the same time:

> *The leading hardware business in Loudonville is carried out by Brown brothers who in 1895 purchased the stock of M Frankiser and Son. The present proprietors are energetic young men, of sterling qualities, and in conducting their business on the cash plan have given their patrons high class goods at low figures and thus established a large trade. Brown Brothers are always referred to as a firm of Loudonville's leading businessmen. With an experience of 11 years in the hardware business, they are prepared to give buyers every advantage possible.[46]*

Fig. 22: Brown Brothers Hardware Store, Loudenville, circa 1895

In 1900, Loudonville (the first syllable is pronounced like the word "loud") was a bustling post-frontier town, an active commercial hub on a railroad line connecting Mansfield with cities to the east. Brown Brothers was one of three hardware stores in town. Raby's, founded in 1885 under the name Whitney and Gaines, is now the only hardware store in Loudonville.

Today, Loudonville is a picturesque village with a population of twenty-six hundred, straddling the Mohican River and nestled in the sizable hills of northeastern Ohio. A Fraternal Order of Eagles office stands where the hardware store used to be, right at the center of town on 140 West Main Street.

A tremendous fire swept through the town on the night of May 2, 1901. It might have been a lamp tipping over in a barn; it might have been a cigarette. At the time, the town had no fire department. Frantic calls went out to Mansfield and Wooster. Wooster floundered, but within minutes, a train pulling a flatcar loaded with Mansfield firemen and firefighting equipment was barreling down the tracks in the dark.

Multiple barns, houses, and businesses burned, including one of the three hardware stores, owned by Frank Young. A barrel of gunpowder inside Young's Hardware exploded, leveling the store.

The Mansfield Fire Department saved the day and most of the town. If Mansfield had not been so well prepared, the whole town center of Loudonville would have burned to the ground that night. Miraculously, there were only a few minor injuries. Brown Brothers Hardware survived.

Among the buildings burned to the ground was the *Loudonville Advocate*, the local newspaper. The *Advocate's* beloved office cat, Tommy, was nowhere to be found among the ashes. Word spread rapidly. Tommy enjoyed special notoriety in the town because, in addition to being a really friendly cat, he was the only cat anyone had ever seen sporting a gold tooth, thanks most likely to a local dentist with a penchant for marketing his services.

Tommy reappeared later looking a little rattled but without a singe. He just needed a little processing time.[47]

In December 1905, the brothers sold the Loudonville store. Hugh, Nora, and their seven-year-old daughter Lucille moved west to Mechanicsburg.

Mechanicsburg, like Loudonville, was a small town located along an important rail line, the Big Four Railroad. Situated about ninety miles southwest of Mansfield and west of Columbus, the town saw a constant stream of visitors from far-away places. Hugh purchased a grain elevator in the middle of town and right on the rail line.[48] The H. M. Brown Grain Company was the center of the action for farmers, townspeople, and travelers.

From the History of Mechanicsburg:

The Brown Elevator has a most advantageous situation on Main Street at the intersection with the Big Four Railroad. It has a large and increasing trade in wheat, corn, oats, clover, and a variety of grass seeds, all kinds of feed, salt, tankage, etc. Coarse grinding and cleaning seed is done.[49]

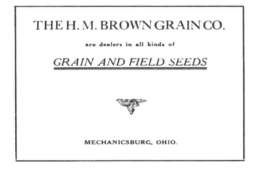

Fig. 23: Mechanicsburg newspaper advertisement, circa 1917

Fig. 24: Mechanicsburg, circa 1900.
The H. M. Brown Grain Company is likely the tall building on the upper left side of the picture.

Chapter 5

Scott Brown

Howard Scott Brown was born on Christmas Day, 1909, in Mechanicsburg. Twelve years younger than his sister, he was a surprise and a miracle for Hugh and Nora. Scott Brown's daughter, Barbara, later wrote:

Grandmother (Nora Steltz Brown) never tired of telling how, on the day father was born, she and grandfather wrapped him in the blankets and laid him under their Christmas tree—"The sweetest, the best, the most beautiful little baby anyone ever saw!..."

In her mind, the miracle of Christmas and the personal miracle of her own son's birth, late in life, after 15 years of marriage, were inextricably intertwined.[50]

Fig. 25: Howard Scott Brown, ten weeks old

Fig. 26: Howard Scott Brown

Howard (who did not adopt his middle name Scott until later) spent his days by his father's side at the H. M. Brown Grain Company. There he got to know and appreciate the full variety of people "from the top rung to the town drunk."[51] Farmers brought their grain for storage, trade, and transport to market. Trains bore businesspeople and passengers from distant places.

Mechanicsburg was also a prime stop for the entertainment circuit.

> *At the turn of the century, culture and entertainment came to Mechanicsburg with the annual Chautauqua, summer circuits of lectures and music in the park. Around 1910 it became known as Matinee Park where many exciting trotting and pacing races were held. Famed speakers such as Mark Twain, Billy Sunday and William Jennings Bryan traveled the Chautauqua circuits, giving rural Americans the chance to hear from the outside world....[52]*

It was the heyday of the traveling show. Everyone watched, at the same time, the same unique event that would never happen quite the same way again, and everyone had their own version of the events to discuss the next day at the H. M. Brown Grain Company.

In 1918, Hugh sold the grain elevator. The family moved to Mansfield, about ten miles north of the Lexington homestead. There, Hugh opened Brown's Drugstore and Soda Shop. Howard was eight years old. Just like at the grain elevator, he joined his father in the soda shop when he was not in school.

The opening of the store coincided with the end of World War I and the building of the Westinghouse factory in Mansfield. Other industries flourished. Demobilization brought workers to the city. In 1924 a new high school was built within walking distance to the store. At first Brown's Soda Shop occupied a leased space, but later it was attached to the house where Hugh and Nora lived.

Barbara Koons, Hugh's granddaughter, describes Hugh:

Fig. 27: Hugh and Nora Steltz Brown

> *Long-boned and thin, with a fringe of white hair and a steady blue gaze, Grandfather was a quiet man who never hurried. He walked slowly, talked slowly, and was methodical in all his habits. Hanging loose on his spare frame, his clothes always seemed slightly too large; baggy trousers, rough fabrics, an itchy wool cardigan with wooden buttons. But his was a sturdy, protective masculine lap; his arms an unassailable haven from whatever terrors, real or imaginary, might be pursuing a child. A deliberate, contemplative man, he lived in rhythm and harmony with life and time passing.*
>
> *In his woodshop were old tools, hand tools, worn to satin by years of palms and fingers gripping, turning. He always carried a pocket knife and liked to whittle, carving things like a chain of links, a ball in a box. His hands were rough, country hands, working hands, with boney fingers. He turned things over and over in his hands, examining, studying, learning.[53]*

Nora was an entirely different character. She was an emotional sprite caught up passionately in the moment. Barbara writes:

> *Pert, bright, brown-eyed, her demeanor and bearing resembled the birds she loved. She fed wild birds in the yard, flapping*

over the grass in apron-flinging frenzies to chase away cats and crows; and she kept tame canaries caged in her kitchen window, where she led their chorus with her own warbling whistle. She could whistle better than most men or boys—clear, bell tones, that rang in harmonies of her own creation.[54]

Barbara continues:

On circus day, she was at the fairgrounds at sunrise to watch the big top go up, and she edged to the front row of spectators at every parade. Her Christmas tree was decorated in early December; Easter eggs boiled and colored by Good Friday. Heart shaped, red sugared cookies were ready early in February, and a carved pumpkin sat grinning on her doorstep at the first hint of frost. But 4 July was her pinnacle.

Beginning at dawn—and surreptitiously throughout the day— she would set off firecrackers. She kept her pockets filled with them. She would sneak out into the yard, set up a string of penny firecrackers, and dash back in the house, trying to look innocent before the popping and banging began.[55]

Fig. 28: Nora Steltz Brown

Brown's Soda Shop was a combination pharmacy, convenience store, and soda fountain. It was well known for Hugh Maurice Brown's invention, Brown's Chocolate Soda, described in the window and on the menu as the "Largest, Coldest and Best Chocolate Soda on Route 30 (including all detours)."[56]

Fig. 29: Nora and granddaughter Barbara

Barbara remembers:

Tall, footed soda glasses were kept in the freezer so they were always frosty. The sodas were made to order with a flair of showmanship. First, ice cream

Fig. 30: Brown's Soda Shop, circa 1940

and chocolate syrup were mixed together in the bottom of the glass. Then a squirt of soda water. Then generous scoops of ice cream, more chocolate syrup, more soda water; hang two "side cars"—scoops of ice cream balanced on the glass rim—top with whipped cream and a cherry, and serve with a straw, a spoon, and a flourish. By the end of World War II, people were coming to the store for those sodas from miles around. [57]

Mansfield was growing. The store was popular. Business was good. Father and son worked side by side.

*   *   *   *   *

Howard sold his first cartoon to the magazine *Judge* when he was ten years old. This was the beginning of his career as a cartoonist. Below are samples of drawings from his teenage years. Figures 31 through 38 on the following pages are all courtesy of the Scott Brown Collection, Billy Ireland Cartoon Library & Museum, Ohio State University:

Fig. 31: Sketchbook, circa 1925

Fig. 32: Sketchbook, circa 1925

Fig. 33: Sketchbook, circa 1925

Fig. 34: Sketchbook, circa 1925

Fig. 35: Drawing, circa 1925

Fig. 36: Drawing, circa 1925

Fig. 37: Sketchbook, circa 1925

Fig. 38: "La Scandler" Lampoon,
front page, circa 1925

Fig. 39: Untitled painting,
circa 1925

Fig. 40: Watercolor, undated

Fig. 41: Oil painting, undated

When Howard was fourteen, he fell into a quarry and shattered his right elbow. The elbow was pinned in a bent position. He could not completely straighten his arm or rotate his wrist ever again.

Howard taught himself to draw with both hands. In just a few months he was back to producing artwork again. His comics appear in every Mansfield High *Manhigan* Yearbook from 1924 to 1927, including the year he broke his arm.

He created these paintings (Figures 42 and 43) less than a year after he shattered his elbow:

Fig. 42: Oil painting, 1925

Fig. 43: Oil painting, 1926

He incorporated his fused right elbow into friendly stances and gestures, as in this picture taken decades later:

Fig. 44: Scott Brown in the Soda Shop, 1964.
© *J. Bruce Baumann – USA TODAY NETWORK*

In school, his grades were poor to terrible, except for A's in Drawing and Writing. He frequently received poor marks in Deportment, defined as "the overall manner in which one conducts oneself."

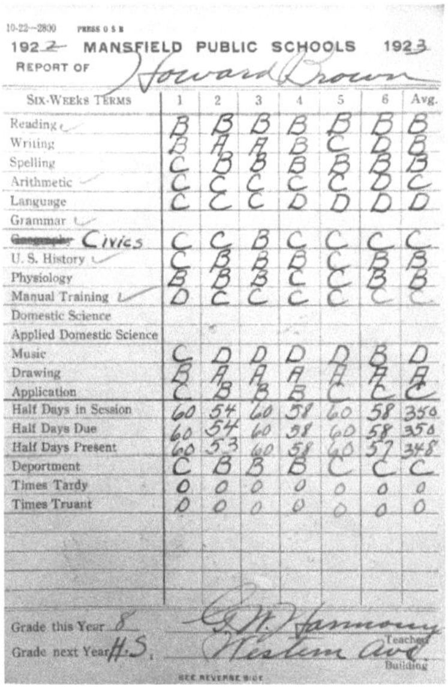

Fig. 45: Eighth grade report card.
Scott Brown Collection, Billy Ireland Cartoon Library & Museum, Ohio State University.

He was mischievous, funny, social, and carefree. In the lampoon *La Scandler* that he created when he was in high school, he wrote "remember, there's a little good in the worst of us and a little bad in the best of us so….be yourself!"[58]

Children and school frequently appeared in his cartoons:

"... and I hope the paper situation eases soon so you can resume issuing grade cards to the children again."

Fig. 46: © SEPS, Licensed by Curtis Licensing, Indianapolis, IN.

"Whenever Dad brings government forms home from the office to fill out I slip in my homework. He does it and doesn't know it"

Fig. 47: Courtesy of Collier's.

"THE MAN WAS SO NICE, HE INVITED ALL US BOYS IN, GAVE EACH OF US A BOTTLE OF POP AND A KITTEN, NEVER EVEN MENTIONED HIS BROKEN WINDOW."

Fig. 48: Original master

"UNDER 'REMARKS' HIS TEACHER WRITES THAT EMPHASIS IS ON CITIZENSHIP, SOCIAL TRAITS, HEALTH HABITS, DEPENDABILITY, GOOD SPORTSMANSHIP, CO-OPERATION, CHEERFULLNESS, EMOTIONAL CONTROL, HONESTY, SAFETY RULES, ATTITUDE. IF WE EXPECT HIM TO LEARN READING, WRITING, SPELLING ETC., WE MUST TEACH HIM HERE AT HOME OURSELVES."

Fig. 49: Pamphlet, The Grade Teacher

Howard graduated from Mansfield High in 1927; his was the first graduating class of the new high school.

Fig. 50: High School Senior Picture, 1927

In the fall of 1927 Howard left Mansfield for the Chicago Institute of Art. At the Institute he realized there was a more established artist named Howard Brown, so he adopted his middle name, Scott. For the rest of his life, everyone knew him as Scott Brown.

Fig. 51: Habeus Corpses, Chicago, 1929

After graduating from the Chicago Institute of Art, Scott went to New York City, where he made connections and refined his craft. In the fall of 1929, the stock market crashed. Broke, Scott Brown returned home to Mansfield, and the corner store.[59] He was nineteen years old.

The following six depression-era cartoons are courtesy of the Richland County Historical Society:

Fig. 52: Detail from a Corner Parade

Fig. 53: Detail from a Corner Parade

Fig. 54: Detail from a Corner Parade

Fig. 55: Detail from a Corner Parade

Fig. 56: Detail from a Famous Firsts

Fig. 57: Detail from a Corner Parade

There was no place better to find humor than Brown's Soda Shop. He said:

> *Really the best advice I could give a beginner would be to get a job in a drugstore and keep his eyes and ears open…. If I weren't working in a drugstore, I'd be loafing in one anyway to get ideas for my cartoons.*[60]

He remembered:

> *One Sunday I was in the front part of the store just looking out the window at trucks, automobiles, sparrows, pigeons, clouds, the man across the street cutting grass….I was just gazing in general when along came a proud father, all full of pep, carrying a large red kite and being trailed by three very happy and exuberant small boys. They were evidently headed for the park, just a couple blocks away, to fly the kite. We got busy then and I had forgotten all about the kite until a little later, when I had occasion to go up to the front of the store after something, and glanced out the window just in time to see the very dejected foursome heading homewards…. minus the kite….*[61]

Fig. 58: Lost kite

And;

> *A lady came rushing in one night for a fast box of Band Aids and a bottle of merthiolate. I asked her what happened. This is exactly what she said:*

"My husband has a basement workshop and a lot of tools sharper than he is."

Fig. 59: © SEPS licensed by Curtis Licensing, Indianapolis, IN.

About six months after the Crash of '29, the first *Corner Parade* poster appeared in the window of the store.

The *Corner Parade* was inspired in part by Billy Ireland's weekly comic page *The Passing Show*. First published in 1908 in the *Columbus Dispatch*, *The Passing Show* entertained readers nationwide for decades. Will Rogers once said; "I take two newspapers, the *New York Times* and the *Columbus Dispatch* for Billy Ireland's page."[62]

Fig. 60: The Corner Parade by Scott Brown, 1930. Courtesy of the Richland County Historical Society.

Fig. 61: The Passing Show by Billy Ireland, 1915. Scott Brown Collection, Billy Ireland Cartoon Library & Museum, Ohio State University.

Banners for two *Corner Parades* follow, courtesy of the Richland County Historical Society:

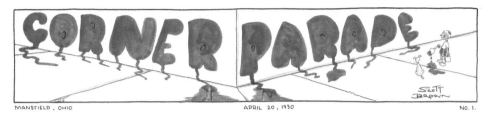

Fig. 62: Banner from the First Corner Parade, April 20, 1930

Fig. 63: Banner from a Corner Parade, April 27, 1930

Famous Firsts

Another series, *Famous Firsts*, appeared regularly in the windows of the store. *Famous Firsts* posters focused on the history of Richland County. The two shown below are also courtesy of the Richland County Historical Society:

Fig. 64: Famous Firsts

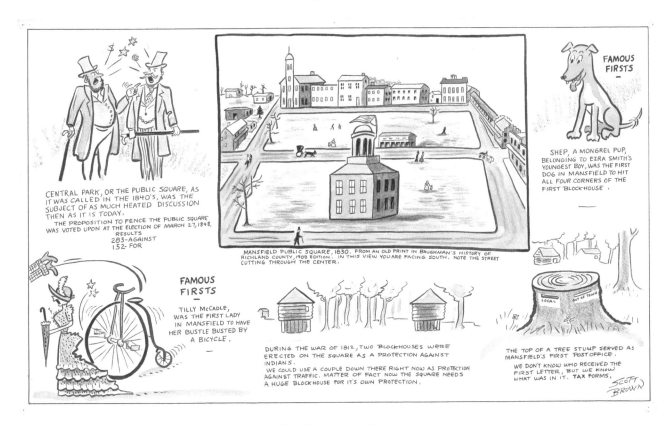

Fig. 65: Famous Firsts

Brown's Soda Shop was not just a convenience store where folks could also get an ice cream or a chocolate soda. It was a place for stories, checkers, gifts, cartoons in the window, and Scott Brown's hand-printed cards for birthdays and other occasions. With a neon sign that simply said "Soda," Brown's Soda Shop was an iconic institution from a unique period in American history.

His daughter Barbara remembers:

The store was small, dim, cluttered; a typical corner store of the era....At the end of the soda fountain, near the front of the store, were the cigar case and cash register. When they weren't busy with customers, grandfather and father would stand behind the cigar case, there they would look out the window and wave to passersby. Grandfather would open the store in the morning, both he and father worked there in the after-noon, spelling each other for meals, and father would close at around 10:30 pm. Then father would come home and work at his drawing board into the wee hours.[63]

Fig. 66: Scott Brown in the soda shop, circa 1944

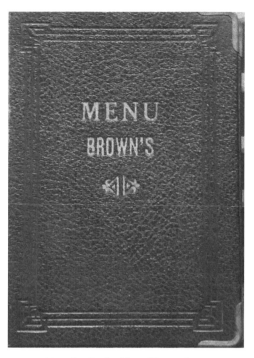

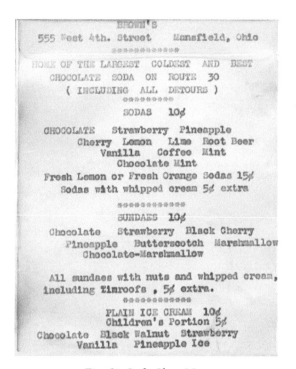

Fig. 67: Soda Shop Menu Cover

Fig. 68: Soda Shop Menu

The soda shop was a popular hangout for all ages. It was in a convenient location and close to the high school. In addition to the world-famous chocolate sodas, the store sold everything from rubber shrunken heads to Chanel No 5. Chuckles, checkers, gag gifts, and sodas were available to anyone who crossed through the corner entrance and passed the wooden Indian next to the door.

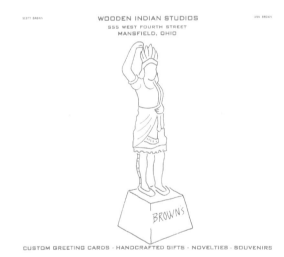

Fig. 69: Over the years two wooden Indians adorned the entrance to the store.

Fig 70: Scott Brown's business name was Wooden Indian Studios.

A reporter describes visiting the store:

> **When I entered the store, Brown was found playing checkers with a customer. A pot of sassafras tea was brewing on a nearby hot plate.**[64]

Something was always going on at the store. Scott Brown wrote the following story for the 1975 *Old Farmer's Almanac:*

Fig. 71: Scott Brown self-portrait, circa 1945, original master

Back in 1955 what started out as a weather gag ended up as one of the strangest and unexplainable things that we ever had happen. The kid brother of one of the high school boys working for me came into the store and had a baby snapping turtle about 1.5" across. I felt sorry for the tiny turtle and proceeded to make a deal with him. For two comic books and a chocolate soda the young snapper was mine. Just for a gag his big brother and I drug out an old aquarium, put gravel on the bottom with sand, placed three large stones, one at each end plus one in the middle. Marked the aquarium in three equal parts with 'Fair,' 'Changeable' and 'Rainstorm.'

Then we put in about 3 inches of water and the turtle, set it on one of our display shelves facing the soda fountain counter, and then proceeded to solemnly tell people that where the turtle would be at six p.m. that is what the weather would be the next day. This first day was on June 23rd, and a nicer day was never underway in this part of Ohio. Barometer was steady, radio and TV forecasters plus the newspapers were all telling what fine weather was in store for the weekend etc, great for picnics…golf… sailing etc….

Matter of fact the only sour note of the day came at six p.m., when the turtle was perched on top of the far end rock of the section marked 'rain…stormy.' Grudgingly we chalked up his first forecast… rain…stormy… and everybody laughed like hell including ourselves. Came three a.m. and there came up a sudden combination goose-downder and gully-washer rain, along with high winds, hail, lots of noise, taking down a few trees plus a few roofs in the area.

To make a long story short the turtle hit it right every day for 14 days before making his first 'miss.' This was on July 7th. We kept the record for a hundred days, and shortly afterward he went into hibernation and eventually passed on to wherever good turtles go after leaving these worldly shores. Out of the 100 days he only missed 15 times. We used to get phone calls every evening from people wanting to know where the turtle was tonight… and we had as many as 40 people in the store at six o'clock to see for themselves. Only part of a theory I have, and it doesn't make sense, is that the tank set straight north and south, and the north end was the stormy one. Why? I don't know and can't even guess."[65]

Sometimes material literally fell into his lap. When sweeping up at the end of the day, he found a small piece of paper on which was written:

One day when I was sad and lonely and sick at heart, I heard a voice saying; "Cheer up, things could get worse."

So I cheered up, and sure enough, things did get worse.[66]

Scott Brown's regular customers contributed enthusiastically. Everybody was looking for a good joke to bring to him. And that was just fine by him! It was no mystery where he got his material. Customers who really got him to chuckle might get a few minutes of fame when their joke or story appeared on a *Corner Parade* or in one of his published comics.

Fig. 72: Anna Von Endt Brown

In 1934 he married Anna (Ann) Von Endt. Ann was a cheerful woman who loved a social gathering and a good cup of coffee with friends. She played violin in the Mansfield Symphony for decades.

Scott and Ann had two daughters; Barbara was born in 1935 and Linda in 1941.

Fig. 73: Anna Von Endt Brown

Fig. 74: Daughters Barbara and Linda with Scott Brown in his studio

Fig. 75: Barbara and Linda Brown

As a child, Barbara often spent the night at Hugh and Nora's house above the soda shop in a small bed in the corner of their bedroom. The corner was nicknamed the Rabbits' Nest, for the Currier and Ives' drawing that hung above the little bed.

MY LITTLE WHITE BUNNIES.
RECEIVING A VISITOR

Fig. 76: "The Rabbits' Nest"

By day, Scott Brown was the spontaneous and pleasant soda shop owner; talking to customers, playing checkers, and listening for a good story. His father was often by his side, and his wife, daughters, and mother passed through frequently. By night, when the world was asleep, the stories of the day would emerge on the cartoonist's page. Often working until dawn, he enjoyed these focused, silent hours alone as much as he did the noise and action of the day. It was a life of exceptional contrast.

Barbara recalls when her father finished his night's artwork, he would sleep until nearly noon.

> *He usually was sitting at the kitchen table having breakfast of Shredded Wheat, canned fruit, coffee, and Camel cigarettes when I came home from school for lunch....While Father was at work, Mother might be playing her violin with friends in a string trio or quartet in our dining room. Our house was filled with paint and ink and paper and color and music; odd meals at odd hours; people sleeping in the daytime and laughing, smoking and talking into the night. It all seemed perfectly normal to me.[67]*

Scottie, as he preferred to be called, was a detailed observer of plants, animals, weather, mushrooms, and people. He spent a great deal of time observing the birds, squirrels, and woolly worms in his own back yard. Every year in November he predicted the number of tracking snows for the year. He claims an Indian gave him the formula—one that unapologetically asks the viewer to suspend all logic:

Scott Brown's Formula for Predicting the Number of Snows in Richland County

add the number of days since the last new moon to the day of the month of the first tracking snow to predict the number of snows for the year.

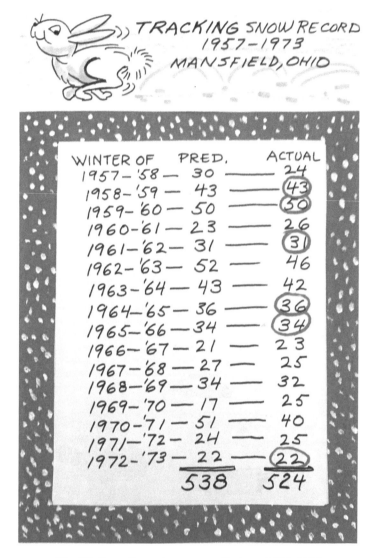

TRACKING SNOW RECORD
1957-1973
MANSFIELD, OHIO

WINTER OF	PRED.	ACTUAL
1957-'58	30	24
1958-'59	43	(43)
1959-'60	50	(30)
1960-'61	23	26
1961-'62	31	(31)
1962-'63	52	46
1963-'64	43	42
1964-'65	36	(36)
1965-'66	34	(34)
1966-'67	21	23
1967-'68	27	25
1968-'69	34	32
1969-'70	17	25
1970-'71	51	40
1971-'72	24	25
1972-'73	22	(22)
	538	524

Fig. 77: Scott Brown's snow predictions, 1958-1973

The criteria for a tracking snow was "clear enough footprints for a nearsighted man to follow in daylight." Sometimes the formula overshot, sometimes it undershot. It was spot on with remarkable frequency. Why? Well, just like that old weather-predicting turtle, Scottie would surely smile and say: "I don't know and can't even guess."[68]

The *Mansfield News Journal* published his snow prediction every year. Dick Goddard, the weatherman for WJW-TV in Cleveland, read his snow predictions on TV. Today, almost forty years after Scott Brown died, two Mansfield residents still use his formula to predict snows—Denny Davis, who worked in the store as a high school student in the 1950s, and Judge Frank Ardis.

Brown's favorite books were *Tom Sawyer* and *Huckleberry Finn*. He was rarely seen without a copy of the *Old Farmer's Almanac* nearby. The article in the 1975 Almanac about the weather-predicting turtle is shown below under the title "A Formula for Short Term Weather Forecasts."[69]

Anecdotes and Pleasantries

A motley collection of amazing stories, useless facts, poor advice and strange news items

A FORMULA FOR LONG-RANGE WEATHER FORECASTS

Alice Hachett of Lake Geneva, Wisconsin, told us about a system of long-range snowstorm forecasting she claims is always "99% correct"—unless it goes haywire which it's done but once in thirty years! She learned it from Frederick Ties of Brohead, Wisconsin, whose great-grandfather learned it in South Dakota from an Indian. It's simply this: count the days from the last new moon before the first snowfall of the year. Then add the date of the month of the first snowfall. The resulting figure is the number of snowfalls there will be during the forthcoming winter. Try it!

A FORMULA FOR SHORT-RANGE WEATHER FORECASTS

Scott Brown, who runs a drugstore in Mansfield, Ohio, wrote us the following not too long ago . . .

"Back in 1955 what started out as a weather gag ended up as one of the strangest and unexplainable things that we ever had happen. The kid brother of one of the high school boys working for me came into the store and had a baby snapping turtle about 1½" across. I felt sorry for the tiny turtle and proceeded to make a deal with him. For two comic books and a chocolate soda the young snapper was mine. Just for a gag his big brother and I drug out an old aquarium, put gravel on the bottom with sand, placed three large stones, one at each end plus one in the middle. Marked the aquarium in three equal parts with 'Fair,' 'Changeable' and 'Rainstorm.'

"Then we put in about 3 inches water and the turtle, set it on one of our display shelves facing the soda fountain counter, and then proceeded to solemnly tell people that where the turtle would be at six p.m. that is what the weather would be the next day. This first day was on June 23rd and a nicer day was never under way in this part of Ohio. Barometer was steady, radio and TV forecasters plus the newspapers were all telling what fine weather was in store for the weekend etc. great for picnics...golf...sailing etc...Matter of fact the only sour note of the day came at six p.m. when the turtle was perched on top of the far end rock of the section marked rain...stormy. Grudgingly we chalked up his first forecast...rain...stormy... and everybody laughed like hell including ourselves. Came three a.m. and there came up a sudden combination goose-downder and gully-washer rain, along with high winds, hail, lots of noise, taking down a few trees plus a few roofs in the area.

"To make a long story short the turtle hit it right every day for 14 days before making his first 'miss.' This was on July 7th. We kept the record for a hundred days, and shortly afterwards he went into hibernation and eventually passed on to wherever good turtles go after leaving these worldly shores. Out of the 100 days he only missed 15 times. We used to get phone calls every evening from people wanting to know where the turtle was tonight... and we had as many as 40 people in the store at six o'clock to see for themselves. Only part of a theory I have, and it doesn't make sense, is that the tank set straight North and South, and the North end was the stormy one. Why? I don't know and can't even guess."

AN UNIMPORTANT, THOUGH INCREDIBLE, ANECDOTE ABOUT JONATHAN SWIFT
by Elmer E. Fisk

Due to their small size and their proximity to the disk of Mars, its two satellites, Phobos and Deimos, were not discovered until 1877. In that year Asaph Hall first observed them with the 26-inch Washington reflecting telescope. Even today, nearly a century later, they can be seen only with the world's larger telescopes under excellent viewing conditions.

How is it then, that, more than a century and a half before Hall's discovery, and a century before these tiny objects (only 10 miles or so in diameter and never closer to Earth than 34 million miles) could possibly have been seen with any telescope yet developed on Earth, their existence was foretold, in writing, by the famous satirist, Jonathan Swift? In Gulliver's Travels, published in 1726, Swift wrote as follows:

"Certain astronomers *** have likewise discovered two lesser stars, or satellites, which revolve about Mars, whereof the innermost is distant from the center of the primary planet exactly three of its diameters, and the outermost five; the former revolves in the space of ten hours, and the latter in twenty-one and a half *** which shows them to be governed by the same laws of gravitation."

Swift had been dead over a century and a quarter before measurements of the orbits of these satellites proved that he had described them with startling accuracy. It was found that Phobos, the inner satellite, revolved about Mars in something less than eight hours, a period which would cause it to appear, to an observer on Mars, to "rise" in the west and "set" in the east, a fact also predicted by Swift.

WHY NOT HEAT YOUR HOME WITH COW BURPS?

"Burping cows must rank as the No. 1 source of air pollution in the U.S.," said the DuPont News last winter. This little tongue-in-cheek

Fig. 78: Old Farmer's Almanac 1975. Used with permission of The Old Farmer's Almanac/Almanac.com.

But wait just a minute! Take a look at the story at the top left, the one he did *not* write, "A Formula for Long-term Weather Forecasts." A woman from Wisconsin describes exactly the method that Scott Brown used for predicting his snow numbers in Mansfield. Coincidence? A joke? Scott Brown in disguise?

We'll never know. But Scott Brown loved tricksters, and the best joke was hidden in plain view.

This love of a good practical joke was inspired in part by Richland County barn painter, carpenter, and artist Seymour Lindsey. Lindsey was a friend of the Browns. Scott Brown tells this story about a joke Lindsey played on his grandfather William Ledlie Brown:

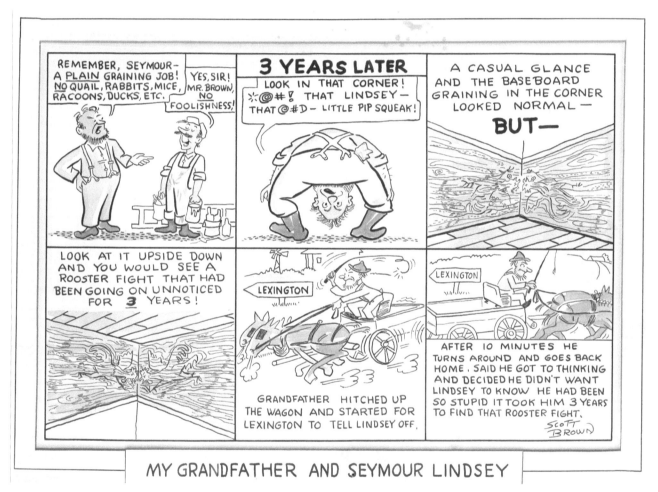

Fig. 79: Courtesy of the Richland County Museum.

Seymour Lindsey was a prolific artist with diverse talent.[70] Below is a portrait of Lindsey by Scott Brown and a few examples of Lindsey's work.

Seymour Lindsey tapped into the same energy with his artwork, barn paintings, and carpentry that Scott Brown brought to those around him with jokes, cartoons, stories, and sodas. Figures 80, 81, and 82 are courtesy of the Richland County Museum.

Fig. 80: Portrait of Seymour Lindsey

Fig. 81: Paper cutout, Seymour Lindsey

Fig. 82: Wooden post detail,
Seymour Lindsey

Fig. 83: Untitled oil, Seymour Lindsey. Courtesy of the <u>Richland Source</u>.

Lindsey appears in two other cartoons by Scott Brown.

Fig. 84: Courtesy of the Richland County Museum.

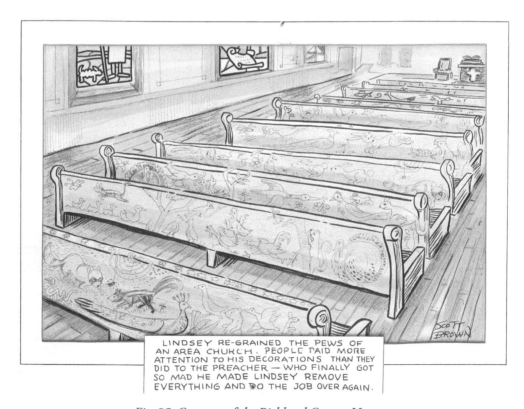

Fig. 85: Courtesy of the Richland County Museum.

Scott Brown created multiple studies for every detail of his comics, as in this frame from the cartoon on page 59. Figures 86, 87, and 88 are courtesy of the Richland County Historical Society.

Fig. 86: Draft

Fig. 87: Draft

Fig. 88: Draft

Fig. 89: Final comic detail.
Courtesy of the Richland County Museum.

Scott Brown celebrated other characters as well, such as Hugh Faulkner, a local handyman:

RATTLE - BANGETY 33 BANG BANG

HUGH FAULKNER

THE BEARDED HANDYMAN OF MANSFIELD FOR MANY YEARS, & HIS CONSTANT COMPANION, A SPANIEL DOG. TO SEE THE TWO CAREENING DOWN PARK AVE. SITTING ON THE GAS TANK OF AN OLD TRUCK CHASSIS WAS A SIGHT NEVER TO BE FORGOTTEN. HE TRADED THE TRUCK IN ON A WHEELBARROW & FROM THEN ON ONLY THE DOG RODE.

Fig. 90: Detail from a Corner Parade. Courtesy of the Richland County Historical Society.

Billy Ireland, Seymour Lindsey, Will Rogers, Mark Twain, Hugh Faulkner, and his own father were influencers that Scott Brown sought out, celebrated, and amplified in the corner store and in his comics.

He worked side by side with his father in the soda shop almost every day for twenty years. In 1949 Hugh Maurice Brown died at home of lung cancer.

Scott Brown ran the store and continued to publish cartoons for decades. His comics not only appeared in the windows of the corner store and in the local newspaper; they were published regularly in *Colliers,* the *Saturday Evening Post,* and *The New Yorker.*

Fig. 91: Scott Brown, circa 1940

Fig. 92: © SEPS Licensed by Curtis Licensing, Indianapolis, IN.

Fig. 93: Laff-A-Day © 1948 King Features Syndicate, Inc.

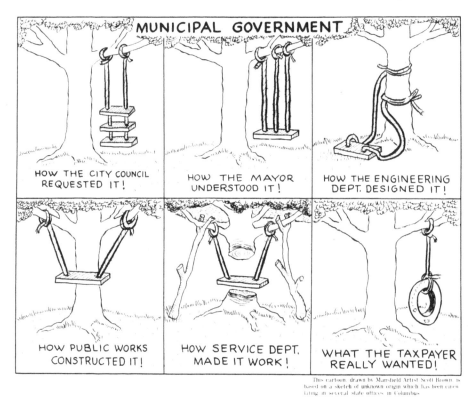

Fig. 94: Courtesy of the Mansfield News Journal.

Scott Brown Collier's

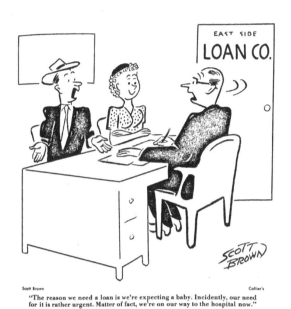

"The reason we need a loan is we're expecting a baby. Incidently, our need for it is rather urgent. Matter of fact, we're on our way to the hospital now."

Fig. 95: Courtesy of Collier's.

Brown Collier's

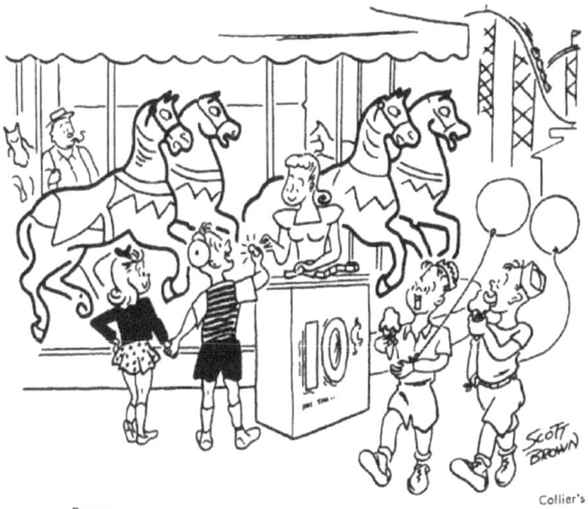

"There's Whitley, blowing it all in on women and horses."

Fig. 96: Courtesy of Collier's.

THE SATURDAY EVENING POST

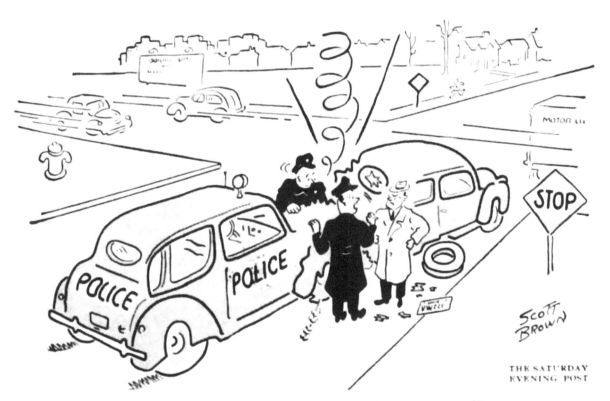

"We thought you weren't going to stop."

Fig. 97: © SEPS Licensed by Curtis Licensing, Indianapolis, IN.

Fig. 98: Original master, later published in the <u>Saturday Evening Post</u>

Fig. 99: Original master

Fig. 100: Original master

Fig. 101: Courtesy of the <u>Mansfield News Journal</u>.

Fig. 102: Original master

Fig. 103: Original master

You never knew where his cartoons might turn up. This one was in the June 1940 *Outdoors Magazine*:

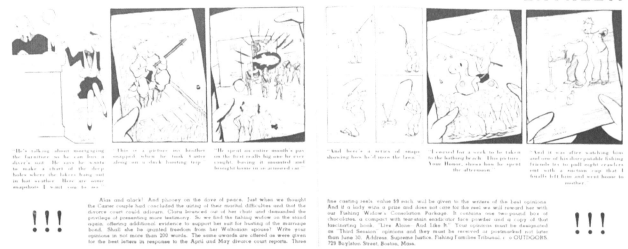

Fig. 104: The fishing widow. Courtesy of the <u>Outdoors Magazine</u>.

Dogs frequently appeared in his comics and artwork.

Fig. 105: Howard Scott Brown,
approx. age fourteen

Fig. 106: Detail from a Corner Parade.
Courtesy of the Richland County Historical Society.

Fig. 107: Oil painting, unknown date.
Scott Brown Collection, Billy Ireland Cartoon Library
& Museum, Ohio State University.

Fig. 108: Oil painting, unknown date.
Courtesy of the Richland County Historical Society.

Fountains and statues appear repeatedly in his work, beginning at a young age. He created the first drawing of a fountain (below left) when he was around age ten.

Fig. 109: Fountain, approximately age ten

Fig. 110: Statue, Put-in-Bay, age fifteen

This undated brooch, about two and a half inches wide, shows Vasbinder Fountain in Mansfield's Central Square. It was most likely a gift for his wife or mother:

Fig. 111: Brooch, oil on wood

The above brooch is the smallest painting he is known to have created. Below is his largest painting, also of Vasbinder Fountain. It measures forty-eight by forty inches.

Fig. 112: Vasbinder Fountain (oil), 1936

Many of the details of this painting are approximated in a linocut he made of Vasbinder Fountain about twenty years later:

Fig. 113: Linocut, Vasbinder Fountain, circa 1958

He added color to the linocut, and this was published as a poster for the 1958 Mansfield Sesquicentennial. The poster was reprinted by the Mansfield Memorial Museum in 2008 in celebration of Mansfield's Bicentennial.

Fig. 114: Linocut with color added, Vasbinder Fountain, circa 1958.
Courtesy of the Mansfield Soldiers & Sailors Memorial Building and Museum.

Exquisite choices of pattern and color, tension and balance are evident throughout Scott Brown's work, such as in this detail from a Corner Parade:

Fig. 115: Detail from a Corner Parade

He experimented in many media. Below are two shallow three-dimensional works. Both are courtesy of the Mansfield Soldiers & Sailors Memorial Building and Museum.

Fig. 116: Johnny Appleseed

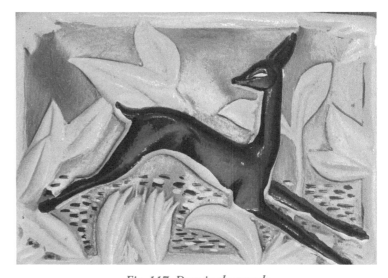

Fig. 117: Deer in the woods

Family members often received greeting cards from him in the mail. Many demonstrated significant planning and execution, like this birthday card for his son-in-law, Ron Mizer:

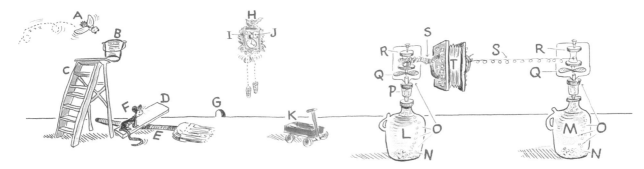

BIG FLY **A** LANDS ON EDGE OF BUCKET **B** ON TOP OF STEPLADDER **C** DELICATELY BALANCED BUCKET FALLS ON BOARD **D** BALANCED ON A BROOMSTICK **E** THROWING MOUSE **F**, (WHO IS WAITING FOR FRIEND **G** TO COME OUT & PLAY TEETER-TOTTER) HIGH IN AIR, LANDING ON TOP OF CUCKOO CLOCK **H**. CUCKOO **I** POPS OUT DOOR **J** CUCKOOING 4 O'CLOCK. THIS FRIGHTENS MOUSE WHO JUMPS, LANDING IN CHILDS TOY WAGON **K**. WAGON THEN SKIDS ACROSS FLOOR SMASHING INTO JUG OF WINE **L**, THE MOUSE, NOT HAVING A SEAT BELT, FLIES OUT OF WAGON & CRASHES AGAINST OTHER JUG OF WINE **M**. IMPACT SHAKES THE **H**— OUT OF THE YEAST **N**, WHICH INSTANTLY STARTS BOTH JUGS FERMENTING LIKE MAD, SENDING GAS BUBBLES **O** UP THRU FERMENTATION LOCKS **P**. GAS COMING OUT OF LOCK TOPS START PROPELLERS **Q** FASTENED TO SPOOLS **R**, REVOLVING— PUSHING & PULLING ATTACHED SPRINGS **S** THAT ARE FASTENED TO ACCORDION **T**, PULLING IT WILDLY BACK & FORTH PLAYING " HAPPY BIRTHDAY TO YOU-RON. & "♪♪♪

Fig. 118: Birthday card, late 1960s

And this birthday card for his daughter, Linda:

MIZER'S OLD PIE CUPBOARD Ⓐ HAD AN OLD PIE INSIDE. OLD MOUSE Ⓒ, GRANDPA OF TEETER TOTTER MOUSE Ⓔ COMES OUT OLD MOUSE HOLE Ⓓ AND CLIMBS INTO OLD PIE CUPBOARD Ⓐ AND BREAKS A COUPLE TEETH Ⓕ NIBBLING THE OLD PIE Ⓑ, THEN ARGUES WITH OLD PIE ABOUT WHICH ONE WAS THE OLDEST. FINALLY THE OLD PIE CUPBOARD GOT INTO THE FIGHT BY CLAIMING IT WAS OLDER THAN THE OLD MOUSE Ⓒ AND THE OLD PIE Ⓑ PUT TOGETHER! THIS OLD RUCKUS Ⓖ MADE SO MUCH NOISE THAT OLD NEIGHBORS Ⓗ CALLED POLICE Ⓘ WHO CAME RIGHT OUT IN OLD POLICE CRUISER Ⓙ. <u>SUDDENLY</u> THE WHOLE OLD GANG Ⓐ-Ⓑ-Ⓒ-Ⓗ-Ⓘ-Ⓙ- REALIZED WHAT DAY Ⓚ IT WAS - AND PROCEEDED TO ALL SING THE OLD-" HAPPY BIRTHDAY SONG---" TO LINDA, WHO COULDN'T HEAR THEM BECAUSE SHE WAS AT THE OTHER END OF THE OLD TOWN, LOOKING AT STUFF IN AN OLD GARAGE, MEANTIME HER OLD LADY Ⓛ & HER OLD Ⓜ MAN SEND HER THE SAME OLD BIRTHDAY WISHES.

Ⓛ LOVE Ⓜ
MOTHER & DAD

Fig. 119: Birthday card, late 1960s

Every Christmas he sent out a Christmas card.

Fig. 120: Christmas card, 1943

Fig. 121: Christmas card, 1940s

Fig. 122: Christmas card. Scott Brown Collection, Billy Ireland Cartoon Library & Museum, Ohio State University.

- 76 -

One Christmas, my sister, brother, and I woke up to handcrafted, working toys from him:

Fig. 123: Handcrafted Toys, 1970s

Christmas was important—but the real big day was Groundhog Day.

Fig. 124: Groundhog Day card, 1967

Fig. 125: Groundhog Day card, 1965

Sketch by Scott Brown

Fig. 126: "Groundhog Day." 1969.
Courtesy of the <u>Mansfield News Journal</u>.

He found something funny every place he looked—including in the mirror. This is how he described his own hospitalization in 1977:

Fig. 127: Gag newspaper from the Soda Shop

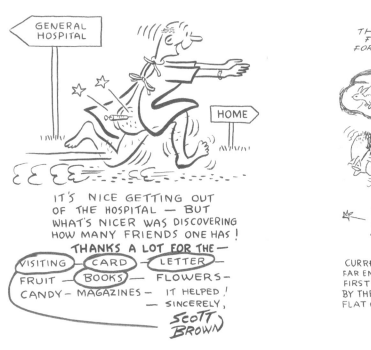

Fig. 128: Thank you card, 1977

Fig. 129: Thank you card, 1977

* * * * * *

The last time I saw my grandfather was in the summer of 1982. I was twenty years old and back from college on the West Coast. He used a wheelchair and wore thick glasses after cataract surgery a few years before. He was comfortable, cheerful, and lucid. He still had his mischievous and welcoming grin.

We were sitting quietly in his room, the windows open, enjoying each other's company and the fragrant summer air. Thundershowers were building. He suddenly looked up with a surprised expression. He pointed at the ceiling in the corner of the room just above the door and said, "Do you see him?"

I looked up to where he was pointing. There was nothing there. "No," I said. "Who?"

"The Angel of Death," he said. He spoke as if an old friend he hadn't seen in a while had just walked into the store.

I looked again. "No, Grandpa, I don't see anything."

He nodded, "Huh," and he grinned. Then he chuckled.

So; you can see the Angel of Death when you are about to die, but the people around you can't.

Well.

That was material for a very funny cartoon.

Fig. 130: Howard Scott Brown
December 25, 1909 - July 14, 1982

Chapter 6

The Largest, Coldest and Best Chocolate Soda on Route 30 (including all detours)

It is the middle of the night. A soft spring rain falls on the farms of Richland County. The resonant song of a train whistle rolls over the land, up the gentle valleys, and out to the sky.

Barbara is tucked into the Rabbits' Nest in Hugh and Nora's bedroom above the Soda Shop. Hugh and Nora are asleep. The windows are open.

Barbara listens to the rain;

> *...a tender, endless lullaby flowed above us, singing down the slate, burbling into the gutters and downspouts, cascading and splashing over the porch, dripping and singing in the maple tree, slicking the street into a black mirror reflecting in peppermint pink the neon SODA glow....* [71]

Just around the corner on Rae Avenue, the street is dark—with the exception of a single golden glow in the window of a small red house halfway up the block on the right. There, to the song of the crickets and the rain, the cartoonist at his drafting table spills the color, chaos, and music of the day onto the next *Corner Parade*.

Fig. 131: Untitled, 1971, by Scott Brown

Acknowledgments

This book is the culmination of three years of research and multiple trips from Seattle to Richland County. Along the way I made more friends than I can count. Each of you has enriched my life and many of you have contributed to this book. I want to specifically thank a few of you.

A huge thanks to Nancy Dunham, descendant of William Ledlie Brown. Many of the facts in this narrative were initially unearthed by you, and far more can be found on the website *www.scottbrowncartoonist.com*. You have an almost mystical ability to find deeds, wills, graves, old newspaper articles, and just about anything else imaginable. My email inbox runneth over. Thanks, Nancy.

Two historians deserve special mention. They are Alan Wigton, the President of the Richland County Historical Society and Robert (Bob) Carter, who wrote numerous books about Richland County history. Alan, thank you for showing me around Richland County to many sites of historical interest. Thanks for helping me focus the narrative, especially regarding the early settlement of Richland County. Thanks for appreciating Scott Brown's work for years, and for your care of many important artifacts, particularly the *Corner Parade* and *Famous Firsts* posters. Bob Carter, thank you for your friendship, insights, and encouragement. Your belief in me was essential to helping me believe in myself as a first-time author. I know that I am far from the first person to be blessed with your mentorship. I enjoyed our time searching through books and documents with you in your study, with an original Seymour Lindsey paper cutting on the wall looking down over us.

To Robert (Bob) Brown, descendant of Robert Carson Brown; thank you for coming down from Cleveland every time I came out to Mansfield from Seattle. Thanks for giving me an excuse to eat at McDonalds. Thanks for the many enjoyable conversations, pleasant days, and for showing me around the Brown homestead where you spent your summers as a child. I will never forget watching the January 6 hearings with you on my laptop in the middle of the Lexington Cemetery, the only place with internet access after the great summer storm of 2022, while we sat among and celebrated our ancestors.

Thank you to my Uncle Ron Mizer. Thanks Ron, for the care you and Aunt Linda took of many family photographs and important artifacts from Scott Brown, many of which made it into this book.

Terry Flaherty, Turas Publishing: How many times did I promise you no more images? No more citations? No more new text? We're done with edits? Your patience has approached infinite, and your input has been absolutely essential. I always looked forward to our Zoom sessions, and always felt grounded and centered after them. This book would have never come together without you.

Thanks to Susan Liberator, director of public relations at the Billy Ireland Cartoon Library & Museum. I know that the fourteen banker's boxes of Scott Brown's cartoons and other artifacts at the Museum are well cared for, and I appreciate your personal involvement and professional help each time I visited.

Acknowledgments - *continued*

Frank Victor, descendant of William Ledlie Brown; thanks Frank, for the many artifacts that you have sent my way, including the first copy we found of *Tears Prayers and Chocolate Sodas*, my mother's unpublished narrative which plays such an important role in the last half of this book.

Thanks to Jeff Mandeville, Curator of the Richland County Museum, for going above and beyond to get the best possible images of several of Scott Brown's comics that are on display at the museum.

Thanks to Scott Schaut, curator of the Mansfield Memorial Museum. Thank you for your early appreciation and support of my grandfather.

Thank you to Kenny Libben, curator of the Cleo Redd Fischer Museum in Loudonville. Thanks Kenny for your efforts to help me on the trail of Hugh Maurice Brown.

To Charlie Wise, author of *Strap Rail into the Woods*; thanks for your lively stories about the early trains, several of which made it into the book, and for tolerating my occasionally incoherent emails.

Thank you, Timothy Brian McKee for your many entertaining stories and images of Mansfield's past.

Thank you, also, to three writers who captured the spirit of Richland County so well; Albert Adams Graham (September 19, 1848 - February 5, 1896), General Roland Brinkerhoff (June 28, 1828 - June 4, 1911), and Dwight Wesley Garber (April 10, 1896 - October 29, 1983).

Thanks to my wife Alice, for bearing the burden and sharing the joy. The days we spent exploring the Richland County countryside together are personal treasures. I will never forget our wonderful time in Loudonville.

Above all, thanks to my mother, Barbara Brown Koons.

Appendix A

Ancestors of Robert and Sara Ledlie Brown

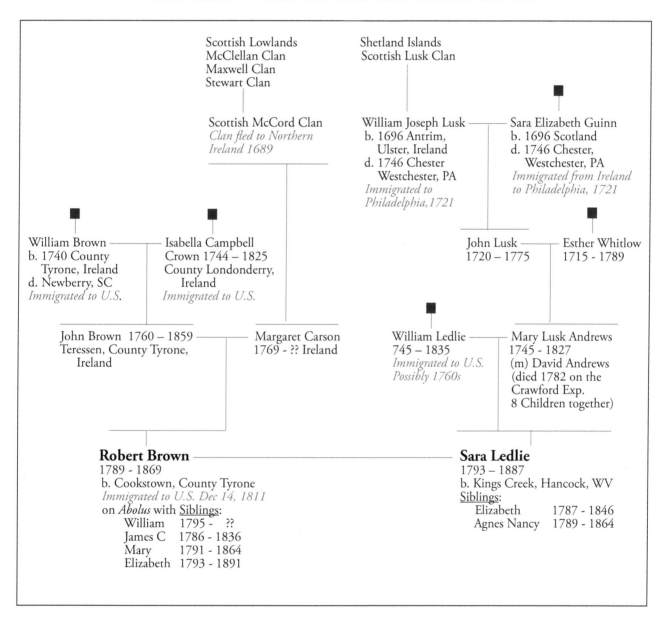

Scottish Lowlands
McClellan Clan
Maxwell Clan
Stewart Clan

Shetland Islands
Scottish Lusk Clan

Scottish McCord Clan
Clan fled to Northern Ireland 1689

William Joseph Lusk
b. 1696 Antrim, Ulster, Ireland
d. 1746 Chester Westchester, PA
Immigrated to Philadelphia,1721

Sara Elizabeth Guinn
b. 1696 Scotland
d. 1746 Chester, Westchester, PA
Immigrated from Ireland to Philadelphia, 1721

William Brown
b. 1740 County Tyrone, Ireland
d. Newberry, SC
Immigrated to U.S.

Isabella Campbell Crown 1744 – 1825
County Londonderry, Ireland
Immigrated to U.S.

John Lusk
1720 – 1775

Esther Whitlow
1715 - 1789

John Brown 1760 – 1859
Teressen, County Tyrone, Ireland

Margaret Carson
1769 - ?? Ireland

William Ledlie
745 – 1835
Immigrated to U.S. Possibly 1760s

Mary Lusk Andrews
1745 - 1827
(m) David Andrews
(died 1782 on the Crawford Exp.
8 Children together)

Robert Brown
1789 - 1869
b. Cookstown, County Tyrone
Immigrated to U.S. Dec 14, 1811
on *Abolus* with <u>Siblings</u>:
    William   1795 - ??
    James C   1786 - 1836
    Mary   1791 - 1864
    Elizabeth 1793 - 1891

Sara Ledlie
1793 – 1887
b. Kings Creek, Hancock, WV
<u>Siblings</u>:
    Elizabeth   1787 - 1846
    Agnes Nancy 1789 - 1864

See **www.scottbrowncartoonist.com** for extensive genealogical information, many more images and further discussion of many of the topics in this book.

Appendix B

The Children and Grandchildren of Robert and Sara Ledlie Brown

Robert Brown 1789 - 1869		Sara Ledlie Brown 1793 - 1887
1. Nancy A. Brown McCune 1818 - 1902 m. Robert McCune *Lexington* Children: John 1848 - 1865 Robert 1850 - 1915 William 1855 - 1930 Richard 1856 - 1921	**2. Margaret M Brown** Hayes 1819 - 1838 m. John Hayes *Indiana* Children: Unknown Name 1837 -?	**3. William Ledlie Brown** 1822 - 1892 m. Eizabeth Ritchie *Lexington* Children: Robert Carson 1851 - 1854 Anne E. 1852 - 1946 Frank Ledlie 1857 - 1915 John Thomas 1859 - 1949 Addie Maggie 1863 - 1865 Edgar Milton 1865 - 1951 Hugh Maurice 1868 - 1949 Charles A 1870 - 1951
4. Sarah Brown Cambpell 1824 - 1869 m. William Campbell *Iowa* Children: William 1848 - 1926 James 1850 - 1922 Sarah 1851 - ?? John 1854 - ?? Arminda 1856 - 1941 Hugh 1860 - ?? Arrilla 1862 - ?? Ann 1862 - 1942	**5. John S. Brown** 1826 - 1907 m. Unity Knox *Iowa* Children: Mary I 1854 - 1905 James L 1856 - 1932 Abby Della 1860 - 1939 John 1864 - 1927 Emma J 1867 - 1945 William A 1870 - 1952 Lela V 1873 - 1963	**6. James Brown** 1830 - 1912 m. Lillith Short *Lexington* Children: Robert M 1858 - 1937 Mary E 1859 - 1929 James S 1861 - 1934 David U 1864 - 1939
7. Mary Brown Adams Watson King 1832 - 1917 m. Thomas Adams Albert Watson Joseph King *Iowa/Montana* Children: Joseph 1860 - 1918 Robert 1862 - 1935 Sherman 1874 - 1888	**8. Robert Carson Brown** 1834 -1898 m. Mary Gailey *Lexington* Children: Helen T 1869 - 1960 Charles G 1874 - 1940	**9. Sara J Montgomery Brown Boals** [adopted 1855] 1850 - 1921 m. Marion Boals *Lexington* Children: Marion 1876 - 1902 George H 1879 - 1901 Infant 1883 - 1883 William R ?? - 1929

Location during adult life in *italics.*

See **www.scottbrowncartoonist.com** for extensive genealogical information, many more images and further discussion of many of the topics in this book.

Endnotes

1. GPS location: 40°37'21.3" N 82°30'17.0"W.
2. Graham, *Richland County*, 286.
3. *Abolus* passenger list. *http://www.familytreecircles.com/passengers-on-the-abolus-newry-to-new-york-1811-35441.html*. The arrival of the five siblings on the *Abolus* is also described in *https://www.genealogy.com/ftm/s/t/o/Tara-Stockton/GENE2-0001.html*: "Robert Brown emigrated from Ireland on the ship *Abolus* on December 14, 1811, with brothers James and William, and sisters Mary Brown Dickson and Elizabeth Brown Duff Downing. The four stayed in Pennsylvania. See note written by Margaret Narmore."
4. Arnold, *History of Loudonville*, 15.
5. Brown, M. G., *Brown Family*, 10.
6. Arnold, *History of Loudonville*, 16.
7. "The Aged Mother of Colonel Robert Brown," *Mansfield Herald*, April 16, 1885, Vol. 35, No. 22.
8. Brinkerhoff, *Pioneer*, 19.
9. Ibid., 23.
10. Ibid., 165.
11. Stanfield, Virgil, "Early Settlers Feared Wild Animals," *Mansfield News Journal*, October 29, 1972, 5F.
12. Ibid.
13. Ibid., Figure accompanies the article.
14. Brown, *Brown Family*, 11
15. Graham, *Richland County*, 240.
16. Ibid., 241.
17. Richland County Museum Website: Round and about the County, *http://richlandcountymuseum.org/round_and_about_the_county*, accessed 10/21/2022.
18. Graham, *Richland County*, 242.
19. Brinkerhoff, *Pioneer*, 150.
20. Graham, *Richland County*, 254.
21. Garber, "'Likker,' and Abe Steltz Start Gold 'Rush.'" *Mansfield News Journal*, April 19, 1964, 65.
22. Ibid., 23.
23. Ibid., 21.
24. Graham, *Richland County*, 235.
25. GPS location: 40°40'45"N 82°32'6"W.
26. Brown, *Brown Family*, 11.
27. Carter, Robert, Personal Communication, 2021.
28. Garber, "Wildcat Banks of Frontier Risky," *Manfield News Journal*, May, 3, 1964, 3.
29. Graham, *Richland County*, 239.
30. Ibid., 239, 257.
31. McKee, Timothy Brian, "The Mohican and Black Fork Canal," May, 3, 2019. *https://richlandcountyhistory.com/2019/05/23/the-mohican-and-black-fork-canal/*, accessed 10/02/2022.

Endnotes - *continued*

32. Garber, "Driskill's Mohican Outlaws Provided Constant Problems," *Mansfield News Journal*, August 11, 1957, 6.
33. Garber, "John Driskill Noted for His Viciousness," *Mansfield News Journal*, September 4, 1957, 40.
34. Garber, "Vigilantes Rifles Ended Driskill's Reign of Terror," *Mansfield News Journal*, October 20, 1957, 10.
35. GPS location: 40°27'02.9"N 80°35'47.8"W.
36. Brooke Co WV Deeds 1797-1901-DB 11, "Transcription of Indenture: Robert Brown to John Crawford," 150, FHL #869817. *https://4d754ece-0338-45b7-99c4-e739545f27b8.filesusr.com/ugd/0b0122_af9a46 0149dc4fa2b90c86d11d7b8fee.pdf,* accessed 10/04/2022.
37. Ibid.
38. Morse, Ellsworth H., Jr. *Richland County, Ohio Original Land Purchases including School Lands*, 11.
39. Graham, *Richland County*, 304.
40. Charlie Wise, personal communication, 2021.
41. Ibid.
42. Barnard, Charles H., Jones, John. F*arm Real Estate Values in the United States by Counties, 1850-1982. https://ageconsearch.umn.edu/record/154628*, accessed on 10/04/2022.
43. Brown, *Brown Family*, 7.
44. Koons, Barbara, *Chocolate Sodas*, 1.
45. Baughman, *A centennial biographical history of Ashland and Richland Counties Baughman*, 796.
46. Arnold, *History of Loudonville,* 504.
47. "Loudonville Swept by a Tempest of Fire," *Mansfield News Journal*, May 3, 1901, 6.
48. Ware, *History of Mechanicsburg*, 58.
49. Ibid.
50. Koons, *Chocolate Sodas*, 13.
51. "Scott Brown anxious to get going again," *Mansfield News Journal*, November 30, 1980, Z-2.
52. Our Towne Mechanicsburg website. *https://mechanicsburgohio.org/history*, accessed 10/05/2022.
53. Koons, Chocolate Sodas, 7.
54. Ibid., 2.
55. Ibid., 3.
56. Brown's Soda Shop menu, personal collection.
57. Koons, Chocolate Sodas, 8.
58. Brown, Scott, *La Scandeler* Pamphlet, unpublished, archived at Billy Ireland Cartoon Museum.
59. Simon, Scott, "Scott Anxious to Get Going Again," *News-Journal*, Mansfield, Ohio, November 30, 1980, 1-B.
60. *The Journal News*, White Plains New York, April 5, 1946, 4.
61. Personal note, Author's collection.
62. Columbus Underground, History Lesson: The Billy Ireland Cartoon Library and Museum, November 14, 2013. *https://columbusunderground.com/history-lesson-billy-ireland-dm1/*, accessed 10/05/2022.

Endnotes - *continued*

63. Koons, *Chocolate Sodas*, 9.
64. *Mansfield News Journal*, April 15, 1957, 11.
65. *1975 Old Farmer's Almanac*, 82-83.
66. *Mansfield News Journal*, June 7, 1957, 17.
67. Koons, *Chocolate Sodas*, 9.
68. *1975 Old Farmer's Almanac*, 83.
69. Ibid., 82-83.
70. McKee, T. B., "Seymore Lindsey Timeless Art From a Distant Time," *https://richlandcountyhistory.com/2019/06/04/seymore-lindsey-timeless-art-from-a-distant-time/*, accessed 10/05/2022.
71. Koons, *Chocolate Sodas*, 16.

Bibliography

Arnold, Henry Hamilton. *Loudonville Illustrated*. Loudonville, Ohio, H. H. Arnold, 1899.

Baughman, A. J. *Centennial Biography History of Richland and Ashland Counties, Ohio.* Chicago, Lewis Publishing Company, 1901.

Brinkerhoff, Roeliff. *A Pioneer History of Richland County, Ohio. Mansfield, OH*: Richland County Chapter, OGS, 1993. (Note: edited by Mary Jane Henney 1993. The original text published as a series of articles in the Ohio Liberal April 9, 1873 to April 9, 1874).)

Brown, Howard Scott. *La Scandeler.* Privately created phamplet, circa 1925.

Brown, Mary G. *A History of the Brown Family with Particular Reference to the Family of Robert Brown of Richland County, Ohi*o. Sharpsburg, PA: Herald Printing Company, 1908.

Eckert, Alan. *The Frontiersmen*. Ashland, Kentucky: Jesse Stuart Foundation, 2001.

Franklin College Board of Trustees. *Franklin College Register: Biographical and Historical.* New Athens, Ohio: West Virginia Printing Company, 1908.

Garber, Dwight Wesley. *Tales of the Mohican Country*.

Graham, Albert Adams. *History of Richland County, Ohio (Including the Original Boundaries) Its Past and Present*. Mansfield, OH: AA Graham & Co, Publishers, 1880.

Herdendorf, Charles E. 2015. B*icentennial History of Sheffield, Ohio–1815-2015*. Sheffield Village Historical Society and Sheffield Bicentennial Commission, Sheffield Village, Ohio, 440 pp.

Hinman, Wilbur. *The Story of the Sherman Brigade.* Alliance, OH: Wilbur Hinman, 1897.

Koons, Barbara. *Night Highway.* Brownsville Oregon: Bedbug Press, 2004.

Morse, Ellsworth H., Jr. *Richland County, Ohio Original Land Purchase including School Lands.* Bellville, Ohio: Richland County Genealogical Society, 1999.

McCullough, David. *The Pioneers*. New York, NY: Simon and Schuster, 2019.

Our Towne Mechanicsburg, *https://www.mechanicsburgohio.org/history*, accessed 10/21/2022.

Reid, Stuart. *Battle of Killiekrankie 1689: The Last Act of the Killing Times*. Yorkshire, England: Frontline Books, 2018.

Richland County Museum website, Round and About the North, *http://richlandcountymuseum.org/round_and_about_the_county*.

Bibliography - *continued*

Ware, Joseph. *History of Mechanicsburg, Ohio.* Columbus, Ohio: FJ Heer Printing Company, 1917.

Webb, Jim. *Born Fighting.* 2nd Edition. New York, NY: Broadway Books, 2007.

Index

A

Abolus, 11
Adams, Thomas, 89
American Revolution, 12
ancestors, 6, 19
Andrews, David, 11, 87
Andrews, Mary Lusk, 87
anti-temperance, 16
Appleseed, Johnny, 17, 72
Ardis, Judge Frank, 52

B

B&O Crossing the Clear Fork, 6
B&O Railroad, 22
Bellville, Ohio, 6, 22, 30
Billy Ireland Cartoon Library &
    Museum, 10, 36, 44, 50, 69, 76
Boals, George H., 89
Boals, Marion (1850?), 89
Boals, Marion (1876), 89
Boals, Sara J. Montgomery Brown, 89
Boals, William R., 89
British, 9, 11
Brook City, West Virginia, 11
Brown Brothers Hardware Store, 30-32
Brown Homestead, 1, 6, 12-14
Brown, Abby Della, 89
Brown, Addie Maggie, 89
Brown, Agnes Nancy, 87
Brown, Ann, 89
Brown, Ann Von Endt, 55
Brown, Anne, 26
Brown, Anne E., 89
Brown, Arminda, 89
Brown, Arrilla, 89
Brown, Charles Alexander, 2, 30, 89
Brown, Charles Gailey, 26, 89

Brown, David U., 89
Brown, Edgar Milton, 25-26, 89
Brown, Elizabeth (1787), 87
Brown, Elizabeth (1793), 87
Brown, Elizabeth (Ritchie), 25-26, 30, 89
Brown, Emma J., 89
Brown, Frank Ledlie, 89
Brown, Helen T., 89
Brown, Howard Scott,1, 3, 5-6, 10, 14, 15-17,
    19, 29, 33, 44, 46, 50, 52-63, 68, 72, 81
Brown, Hugh (1860), 89
Brown, Hugh Maurice (1868), 1, 25-27, 29, 89
Brown, James, 11-12, 89
Brown, James C., 87
Brown, James L., 89
Brown, James S., 89
Brown, John (1760), 87
Brown, John (1848), 89
Brown, John (1854), 89
Brown, John (1864), 89
Brown, John S., 22, 89
Brown, John Thomas, 30, 89
Brown, Helen, 25
Brown, Lela V., 89
Brown, Margaret M., see Hayes, Margaret M.
    (Brown)
Brown, Margaret M., 12
Brown, Mary (1791), 87
Brown, Mary (1832), see King, Mary (Brown)
    Adams Watson
Brown, Mary E., 89
Brown, Mary (Gailey), 19, 26, 89
Brown, Mary I., 89
Brown, Nancy A., see McCune, Nancy A. (Brown)
Brown, Nora Steltz, 29-30, 32-35, 55, 83
Brown, Robert (1789), 1, 11-14, 18-19, 20,
    22-23, 25, 87, 89
Brown, Robert (1848), 89
Brown, Robert (1850), 89

Index - *continued*

Brown, Colonol Robert Carson (1834), 22, 25, 89
Brown, Colonol Robert Carson (1851), 22, 25, 89
Brown, Robert M., 89
Brown, Sara J. Montgomery, see Boals, Sara J.
   Montgomery Brown
Brown, Sara Ledlie, 1, 11-14, 18-19, 21-22, 25,
   30, 87, 89
Brown, Sarah (1851), 89
Brown, Sarah (1824), see Campbell, Sarah
   (Brown)
Brown, William (1740), 87
Brown, William (1795), 87
Brown, William (1848), 89
Brown, William (1850), 89
Brown, William (1855), 89
Brown, William A. (1870), 89
Brown, William Ledlie, 19, 25-26, 30, 59, 89
Brown's chocolate soda, 1, 5, 35, 52-54
Brown's Drugstore and Soda Shop, 34-35, 49, 52

C

Campbell, Sarah (Brown), 89
Campbell, Isabella, 87
Campbell, James, 89
Campbell, William, 89
canals, 20-23
Carson, Margaret, 87
cartoonist, 1, 36, 56, 83
Chicago Institute of Art, 46
Christmas, 33, 35, 77
Christmas cards, 74-76
Civil War, 22, 25, 30
Clear Fork River, 6, 9-110
Collier's, 45, 65
Columbus Dispatch, 50
Corner Parade, 47-48, 50-51, 55, 63, 68, 72, 83
Crawford Expedition, 11
currency, 16, 19

D

Davis, Denny, 57
depression-era, 47
derailments, 23
descendants, 25
drawing, 14, 36, 39, 44, 52, 55, 69
Driskill-Brody gang, 21

E

Euro-American, 6, 10

F

Famous Firsts, 17, 48, 51-52
financial collapse of 1819, 20;
   of 1837, 21, 23

G

Gailey, Mary, see Brown, Mary (Gailey)
Goddard, Dick, 57
Greenville Treaty Line, 9, 12
Greenville Treaty of 1795, 12-13
gristmill, 9-11, 16, 19
Groundhog Day, 78-79
Guinn, Sara Elizabeth, 87

H

H. M. Grain Company, 1, 32-33
Hayes, John, 89
Hayes, Margaret M. (Brown), 12, 89
history of Richland County, 15, 30, 51

I

immigrants, 11
Indian country, 9
Ireland, Billy, 50, 63

K

King, Joseph (184?), 89
King, Joseph (1860), 89
King, Robert, 89
King, Sherman, 89
King, Mary (Brown) Adams Watson, 89
Kings Creek, 11-12, 21-23
Knox, Unity, 89
Koons, Barbara Brown, 29, 33-35, 52, 55-56, 83

L

La Scandler, 41,44
land grant, 12, 22
Leedy, John, 13
Ledlie, Agnes Nancy, 87
Ledlie, Elizabeth, 87
Ledlie, Mary (Lusk) Andrews, 11, 21, 87 Ledlie, Sara (1793), see Brown, Sara (Ledlie)
Ledlie, William, 11, 22, 87
Lexington, Ohio, 9-10, 21-22, 25, 34, 36, 42, 46, 57-58
Lindsey, Seymour, 59-63
linocut, 3, 71
Loudenville, Ohio, 31
Lusk, John, 87
Lusk, Mary, see Ledlie, Mary (Lusk) Andrews
Lusk Scottish Clan, 87
Lusk, William Joseph, 87

M

McClellan Clan, 87
McCord Scottish Clan, 87
McCune, Nancy A. (Brown), 12-13, 89
McCune, Robert, 89
Maxwell Clan, 87
Mansfield, Ohio, 1, 5, 9, 12-13, 15, 20-23, 29-32, 34
Mansfield Bicentennial (2008), 71

Mansfield Central Square, 70
Mansfield High *Manhigan* Yearbook, 42
Mansfield High School, 46
Mansfield Memorial Museum, 71-72
Mansfield News Journal, 44, 57, 67, 79
Mansfield Sesquicentennial (1958), 71
Mansfield Symphony, 55
Mechanicsburg, Ohio, 1, 32-34
Mingo Bottom, 12
Mizer, Linda Brown, 55, 73
Mizer, Ron, 73
Mohican and Black Fork Canal, 21
Mohican River, 31

N

Native Americans, 6
New Philadelphia, 12
New Yorker, The, 63
Newry, Ireland, 11

O

Old Boundary Line, 9
Ohio frontier, 10-11
Ohio River, 6, 11-12, 20-23
one-hundred-sixty acres, 11, 22
Overland Trail, 20

P

painting, 5-6, 41-43, 60, 69-71
Paris, Ohio, 15
Passing Show, the, 50
pioneer history, 1
Pittsburg, Pennsylvania, 11
Philadelphia, Pennsylvania, 11
predicting the number of snows, 56-58
Presbyterian, 11, 26, 30

Index - *continued*

R

Rabbits' Nest, 55-56, 83
Richland County, Ohio, 6, 9, 11-16, 18-25, 30, 51, 56, 59, 83
Richland County brigands, 21
Richland County Historical Society, 13, 49-51, 62-63
Richland County Museum, 59-62
Richland Source, 9, 20
Ritchie, Elizabeth, see Brown, Elizabeth (Ritchie)

S

Sandusky, Mansfield and Newark Line, 1, 22-23
Saturday Evening Post, 45, 49, 63-65
sawmills, 9-10, 16
Scots-Irish, 11
Short, Lillith, 89
sketches, 36-38
snakes, 13-14
Steltz, Abram, 16-17, 30
Steubanville, Ohio, 12
Stewart Clan, 87

T

trains, 6, 21-23, 31, 34, 83
transportation, 6, 20-23
Tuscawaras Valley, 12

V

Vasbiner Fountain, 70-71

W

War of 1812, 1, 9-10, 12, 15-16, 20, 23
Washington and Monroe Temperance Society, 16
watercolor, 41
Watson, Albert,
Watson, Amariah, 9-11, 19

Watson's Mills, 11-12, 19
Weavor, Catherine, 16
Weirton, West Virginia, 11
whiskey, 15-16, 18-19
Whitlow, Esther, 87
Wildcat Banks, 19
wooden Indian, 5, 53
Wooster, Ohio, 12, 31

About the Author

Christopher A. Kuntz is an eye surgeon and outdoors enthusiast. He lives with his wife in the hills just east of Seattle, where he spends his time trying to keep up with his children.

He can be reached at *scottbrowncartoonist@gmail.com*.

Fig. 132: Christopher A. Kuntz